The author's palpable excitement about his message gives the impression that his words leaped onto the pages just moments before these two volumes went to press. This is not soothing but bracing fare, fare for those seeking a deeper faith life, a life of "just living" in the wholeness of the New Covenant of the Spirit for which we were created and redeemed and by means of which the world will take notice . . . and begin to wonder at what it sees in us. —CONNIE WOOLDRIDGE, author of *The Brave Escape of Edith Wharton*, a New York Times Critics Choice

Wholeness: Where God Is Bringing Us is the result of decades of deep rumination on a few life-altering truths. My friend, Bruce Weatherly, has marinated his mind on a number of cherished passages in God's Word for a very long time, personally experiencing freedom and joy, and is now sharing his discoveries with us. I recommend reading *Wholeness* as it was written—in snatches, over time, and with much reflection. —MATTHEW C. MITCHELL, Pastor of Lanse Evangelical Free Church and author of *Resisting Gossip: Winning the War of the Wagging Tongue*

Bruce conveys the essence of the beauty and power of God's truth about our freedom in Christ. You'll be excited to walk into your next moments with Jesus as you grow in a deeper understanding of walking in the Spirit. —JON BURCHARD, Licensed Professional Counselor, Founder/Ambassador, In Him Christian Wellness, Lemoyne, PA

My dear friend Bruce Weatherly has written *Wholeness* out of a life that has been touched by and devoted to the reality of the Spirit of God in him. Bruce's heart is that we might live into the reality of God's Spirit within us and our union with Christ, our "oneness" with God. We are the branches and the Lord is our vine, and as we abide in him—just abide in him—we will be the fruit-bearers we were made to be. — PETER ROWAN, Pastor of Second City Church (PCA), Harrisburg, PA

In *Wholeness*, Bruce Weatherly invites readers into the profound simplicity of the gospel: Christ in us, doing through us what we cannot do ourselves. As a clinician, I see the longing for peace, identity, and purpose in so many lives—and this book speaks directly to that ache. It's not a self-help manual; it's a Spirit-led call to freedom, oneness, and joy in Christ. Read it slowly. Let it sink in. It just might change how you live. —ERIK L. SUNDQUIST, LCSW-C, CEO and Founder, Safe Harbor Behavioral Care

I do 100 percent endorse Bruce Weatherly's *Wholeness*. Dr. Weatherly has put all my questions about growth and how to walk in the power of the Holy Spirit in one scripture-packed homily that says it all and answers all questions. —DEAN OVERHOLT, Ordained Minister with the Evangelical Free Church of America (EFCA) since 1986; career missionary to Asia with the EFCA International Mission (Retired)

This is an earnest plea to abide in Christ as He abides in us through the Holy Spirit. *Wholeness* is a rich treasure of Bruce's rigorous study of scripture and explanation of the role of the Holy Spirit in the life of a disciple of Jesus. Extensive quotes from Christian leaders illuminate what is being taught. I highly recommend this book for deep reflection on the life of Christ in us. —DEWY WETHERBY, Executive Director of Global Avenues Ministries, Colonial Beach, VA

In *Wholeness*, Bruce Weatherly writes, "The righteous requirements of the law are fully met *in* us, not *by* us." My heart cries, "Amen!" The Christian life is just living the life that Christ is living in us. Weatherly's book is a corrective for all of us who dwell on our own shortcomings and sins. Read it devotionally and you will find that your eyes are turned from yourself toward Jesus, the only one who can truly live this Christian life. —DALE KULP, Pastor, Honorably Retired, Presbyterian Church in America (PCA)

I have been fortunate enough to know Bruce, who is a licensed psychologist as well as having more of the Bible memorized than anyone else I know, for a number of years, and I will happily say that my internal thought life, my parenting and marriage, and my ministry are all far better because of the time I've spent with him. Bruce's ideas are a useful corrective for the trap of the morbid, anguished way of living we can fall into. This book can be read quickly, like an invigorating shower, or devotionally dwelt in, like a relaxing bath. Either way, you'll get good results. —JEDIDIAH STALKER, pastor in training, under care of the Susquehanna Valley Presbytery of the Presbyterian Church in America (PCA)

Volume 1

WHOLENESS

Where God Is Bringing Us

BRUCE WEATHERLY

BROOKSTONE
PUBLISHING GROUP
Birmingham, Alabama

Wholeness, volume 1

Brookstone Publishing Group
An imprint of Iron Stream Media
100 Missionary Ridge
Birmingham, AL 35242
IronStreamMedia.com

Library of Congress Control Number: 2025911368

Cover design by twolineSTUDIO.com

ISBN: 978-1-960814-18-0 (paperback)
ISBN: 978-1-960814-19-7 (eBook)

1 2 3 4 5—29 28 27 26 25

To Donna, my wife for more than forty years and the woman I love more and more each day. We are truly and literally a match made in heaven. Thank you for being you.

Contents

Acknowledgments

First, I thank my wife, Donna, the sweetest, gentlest, most selfless person I know. Her hours and days of dealing with the countless irritating details, stressful surprises, and mundane duties of everyday life in our home made it possible for me to write, review, revise, and meet deadlines. In many ways Donna has postponed, and even sacrificed, her own creative energies so that I could produce these two volumes. These pages are as much a labor of love on her part as on mine.

I would like to thank Iron Stream Media / Brookstone Publishing. They are a team of excellent, efficient, and gracious planners, coordinators, and editors. Specifically, I am grateful for the help and encouragement of John Herring, CEO, and Kennedi Shoulders, Assistant, in the early days of this project. Ann Tatlock and Susan Cornell were wonderful and rewarding to work with in the editing process. Michele Trumble kept me abreast of practical and financial matters as well as coordinating the fun process of cover design. Thank you, as well, to all the behind-the-scenes gifted men and women at Iron Stream for whom I have no names.

Much appreciation for my manuscript readers who gave such helpful suggestions, insights, and encouragement: Pastor Matt Mitchell, Pastor Dale Kulp, Jon Burchard, Erik Sundquist, Dean Overholt, Connie Wooldridge, Jed Stalker, Dewy Wetherby, and Pastor Peter Rowan.

Steven Robinson designed a beautifully informative one-sheet for me. This 8½-x-11 semigloss was a significant contributor in "selling me" to my publisher. My son, Nate Weatherly, took my scribbles and magically formed them into the book-ready Romans 6 diagram, an integral explanatory component found in both volumes of *Wholeness*.

I am grateful for all in my life who have encouraged and prayed: my son and daughter-in-law, Nate and Sheila; my daughter and son-in-law, Missy and Jed Johnson; my son and daughter-in-law, Steve and Tirzah Gibboney, and my oldest granddaughter, Lisa. I have deepest appreciation for my church, Second City Church, in inner city Harrisburg, Pennsylvania. My small-group Bible study has been meeting weekly for eight years to pray, learn, and fellowship. I have deep affection for and joyfully appreciate each of you—Chris, Steve, Aaron, Amber, and Christian. I know there are others I've neglected to mention, who prayed for me and the book. God knows you, and I thank you.

I've certainly learned much from the vast array of clients I've counseled with over the past thirty-six years. In the context of listening to them, speaking to them, thinking about them, and praying for them, I've become more and more convinced of what I've written in the pages that follow. The Bible holds the answers to the deepest needs of the human heart. If any of you are reading this, I thank you for trusting me, confiding in me, and being humbly teachable, even and when I got a bit intense and direct.

I'm so very appreciative of my mentors, many of whom died about three or four hundred years ago. I certainly look forward to listening to them, speaking with them, fellowshipping with them, partying with them, and thanking them in person in heaven and on the New Earth. Thank you for your Holy Spirit–led words of wisdom and truth: François Fénelon, Jeanne Guyon, Augustine, John of the Cross, Jean-Pierre de Caussade, John Owen, Julian of Norwich, Blaise Pascal, Martin Luther, Matthew Henry, Charles Spurgeon, and more "recently": Andrew Murray, A. W. Tozer, Larry Crabb, L. E. Maxwell, John Piper, F. J. Huegel, James Strong, Howard Blandau, and Howard Hendricks. Your books and sayings have deeply affected and shaped me for Jesus.

I have six grandkids who have provided fun-filled breaks, some bumps and bruises, and some great anecdotal material for this book. Thank you Lisa, Lucy, Hank, Arlo, Amos (Moose), and Betty. Watching you grow and being with you is so good for my soul.

Finally, Father, Son, and Holy Spirit, I thank you for speaking to me and causing me to see precious truth in Your Word, the Holy Bible. Jesus, Son of God, You are certainly treasure hidden in a field. To find You and know You is life and freedom indeed. Thank You for our book.

Introduction

In October 1970, about six weeks into my freshman year at college, a couple of guys from a campus ministry came to my dorm room and shared the gospel with me through a little yellow booklet. Only a few days later, alone in my room late at night while lying in bed, I put my faith in Jesus Christ for the forgiveness of all my sins. I asked Him to come into my heart and rule there from that moment on. I was only too happy to have Jesus come into me, take control of my life, and live His life through me, having become poignantly aware that I was incapable of living my life in any way that brought peace and contentment.

Waking up the next morning, remembering what I had done the night before and sensing a new Presence, I felt clean, happy, and free. I had found the Truth! (John 14:6). All was not "meaningless" (Ecclesiastes 1:2) after all!

In the days that followed, I began going through inward and outward changes. I found myself liking people and wanting to do things to help them. I started going to meetings held by this campus ministry. I enjoyed the people and learned a lot. I began reading and studying the Bible.

Pretty soon I learned from these people that I should be "going out witnessing." Actually, there was quite an emphasis on this. Me being me, I gradually got "under the law" about this witnessing thing. I made myself do it and even saw results. I felt guilty about not feeling like doing it. I began to lose my joy. Joy and freedom were being replaced by guilt and compulsion. I was running well but hindered myself. (See Galatians 3:3). After beginning with the Spirit, I resorted to trying to attain my goal by human effort. I embarked upon a journey of inward struggle that lasted many years. It all happened so subtly.

What follows in these pages is the Bible's solution to this all-too-common problem of what can be called the "Galatians syndrome." This syndrome is characterized by the believer trying to attain righteousness through works rather than by faith. Scripture holds the cure for all Christians, young and old, who, having begun in the joy and freedom of the Spirit, now find themselves trying to attain their goal by human effort. The cure is glorious. The cure is spiritual and comes from God Himself.

The Western church needs to rediscover the role of the Holy Spirit in living the Christian life. We need to more frequently hear and more deeply understand Paul's teaching regarding living by the Spirit (Galatians 5:16). We do not fully understand Paul and his message until we come to recognize him as the excited herald of the New Covenant of the Spirit (2 Corinthians 3:5–6).

In *Wholeness: Where God Is Bringing Us*, we'll look at the scriptural truth of oneness with Christ, but we won't stop there. What are some of the faith-challenging implications of our oneness with Christ and what do we do with them? We sing songs about being one with Christ, free, whole, restful, and fruitful, but how true are these in our daily experience? Can they be? They can, and it's not by effort and continual head struggle. We've already tried that.

Let me give you a little taste of what follows in these pages. In John 8:31–38, Jesus is speaking to Jewish leaders who are questioning Him. He says if they hold to His teaching, they are really His disciples and they will come to know the truth and the truth will set them free. Later, in verse 36, Jesus says to them, "So if the Son sets you free, you will be free indeed" (ESV).

What is the truth they will come to know that will set them free if they hold to His teaching? In the context we see that Jesus is talking about freedom from sin (vv. 34–36). What we will see in the pages that follow is that Jesus is talking about three things— freedom from sin as a way of life, freedom from the law, and "freedom indeed"—freedom to just live and be myself and to see myself becoming more and more like Jesus (Galatians 5:22–23). All of this happens as I'm simply living, simply abiding in the Vine.

If Jesus is living in me, and He is (Galatians 2:20), and if He's controlling me, and He is (Romans 8:9), then I'm free—free from sin as the norm in my life, free from the law, and free indeed, free to just live and be myself (wholeness) while growing in righteousness at the same time. Jesus is living in me now, and He's controlling me now in the New Covenant of the Spirit (Ezekiel 36:26–27). God is bringing us into knowledge of this wholeness. Jesus said so (John 8:32). The truth that sets us free is knowing the New Covenant of the Spirit. Let's begin learning, knowing, feeling, seeing, and realizing it together.

– PART 1 –

The New Covenant
of the Spirit

– 1 –

God's Plan to Reach the Nations

EZEKIEL 36:22–29; 37:14

God is not looking for people to work for Him but people who let Him work mightily in and through them.

—John Piper

Let's begin simply by reading together the scriptures from Ezekiel:

Therefore say to the house of Israel, "This is what the Sovereign LORD says: It is not for your sake, O house of Israel, that I am going to do these things, but for the sake of my holy name, which you have profaned among the nations where you have gone. I will show the holiness of my great name, which has been profaned among the nations, the name you have profaned among them. Then the nations will know that I am the LORD, declares the Sovereign LORD, when I show myself holy through you before their eyes.

"For I will take you out of the nations; I will gather you from all the countries and bring you back into your own land. I will sprinkle clean water on you, and you will be clean; I will cleanse you from all your impurities and from all your idols. I will give you a new heart and put a new spirit in you; I will remove from you your heart of stone and give you a heart of flesh. And I will put my Spirit in you and move you to follow my decrees and be careful to keep my laws. You will live in the land I gave your forefathers; you will be my people, and I will be your God. I will save you from all your uncleanness." (Ezekiel 36:22–29)

I will put my Spirit in you and you will live, and I will settle you in your own land. Then you will know that I the LORD have spoken, and I have done it, declares the LORD.

(Ezekiel 37:14)

God's Gracious Way

We see that God's plan is now and has always been to show Himself holy through His people before the eyes of a watching world. It is crucial that we see this word *through*, for this truth is central to understanding the New Covenant of the Spirit.

It is significant that a prominent feature of this New Covenant is the importance of God's people and the nations recognizing that God Himself is doing all this because He chooses to. We see that the Lord is working out a plan and has a specific purpose for implementing what Paul calls the New Covenant of the Spirit (2 Corinthians 3:4–6). God's purpose is to glorify Himself before the nations, that the nations would know that He is the Lord because He has shown Himself holy through His people. This has always been God's purpose for His people. This is God's purpose for the church, for all believers, for us right now. "Then the nations will know that I am the LORD . . . when I show myself holy through you before their eyes" (Ezekiel 36:23). This is God's purpose for you and me right now, to allow Him to show Himself holy through us moment by moment, day by day, as we live our lives here on earth wherever He has placed us.

It is of great importance and concern to God that (1) the nations know that He is the Lord (36:23) and (2) that His people, those into whom God has put His Spirit (36:27, 37:14), the true church of God, know that He is the one who does it (37:14). It is important to God that we come to know that the Christian life is God Himself coming to live inside of us and then living His life through us as we just live. It is important to God that we come to know that it is all Him. And it is important to God that we come to know this New Covenant of the Spirit both theologically and experientially.

> *Unbelieving people will only be attracted to Him as we are living holy and supernatural lives.*

What does the word *it* mean in Ezekiel 37:14 when it says that He is the One who has "done it"? Consider this:

It = everything . . . God showing the holiness of His great name, reaching and convincing the nations that He is the Lord, so that we know He is the one doing it. The way God wills to do these things is by putting His Spirit in us and doing "it" through us as we just live (37:14).

It = God Himself doing everything it takes for the nations to know that He is real and He is the Lord.

It = God Himself doing everything it takes for us to know that He is the one doing it, by putting His Spirit in us and living His life through us (36:23).

Coming to understand, believe, and live according to God's promise in the New Covenant of the Spirit is crucial if the church is to be effective in these last days. It is only by God Himself doing His will and good work through us, and the nations thereby seeing that it is Him living through us, seeing by our words and actions that we have "been with Jesus" (Acts 4:13), that the Lord gets all the glory. God wants it this way. God wills to do it all Himself through us because, by His getting all the glory, unbelieving people will fear Him and be attracted to Him and only Him. Unbelieving people will only be attracted to Him as we are living holy and supernatural lives. The only way this happens is by His living through us as we just live. (See also 1 Corinthians 2:1–5.)

Our Impotence, His All-Sufficiency

We read that, contrary to how God wanted them to be a light to the world, Israel has profaned God's holy name before the nations. In the flesh and by their own efforts, no matter how well intentioned they have been at times, they have ended up profaning God's holy name before the nations rather than glorifying it. They have not been able to live holy lives. It is going to take God Himself living through them. Then, and only then, will the nations know that our God is the Lord. This is all just as true for us, the church, living among the nations today. We are no more capable of showing the holiness of His great name than was Israel.

In these nine verses God says, "I will," eleven times. If God Himself doesn't do it, it's not going to happen. As A. W. Tozer put it, "For true faith, it is either God or total collapse."[1] The only way the nations are going to know that God is the Lord is, as Andrew Murray states, by entering into His people "in divine power, to give and be in them what He [has] taught them to desire."[2]

In his book *Humility*, Murray says this, "All Christ's teaching of His disciples, and all their vain efforts, were the needful preparation for His entering into them in divine power, to give and be in them what He had taught them to desire."[3]

We all need to have this same experience of failure by our own efforts and, as a result of this painful failure over and over again (Romans 7:14–25), we come to the place of utterly depending on His living in us to give and be in us what He has taught us to desire. We must come to know through our own experience that if God doesn't do it, it's not going to happen—that it's either God or total collapse. This needs to become the faith and level of faith by which we live moment by moment, day by day. And this is where God is bringing us by grace through faith.

> *God must literally enter into us to do in us, for us, and through us what we cannot do.*

We ourselves are no more capable of getting there than we are of being there.

Please notice that what God is saying in Ezekiel 36:26–27 is identical to what Andrew Murray is saying in the above quote. Murray's statement is the New Covenant of the Spirit and this, likewise, must be the experience of and the lesson learned by Christ's followers today if we are to affect and change the world around us in a lasting way. "You did not choose me, but I chose you and appointed you to go and bear fruit—fruit that will last. Then the Father will give you whatever you ask in my name" (John 15:16).

Jesus's words here are in the context of teaching His disciples the lesson of the Vine and branches (John 15:1–8), which we will look at in more detail later. Suffice it to say for now that it is a lesson regarding the truth that in order to bear fruit, the life of the Vine must flow through the branches, which are us. There's that word again, *through*, as true today as it was in the days of Ezekiel and the apostles. "Then [and only then] the nations will know that I am the LORD, . . . when I show myself holy through you before their eyes" (Ezekiel 36:23).

The New Covenant of the Spirit is God's way of fulfilling His plan and purpose to glorify Himself before an unbelieving world. Howard Hendricks, in his book *Elijah: Battle of the Gods*, states,

"How do you convince a world that God is alive? By His aliveness in your life, by His work in producing reality in your experience. What a message for a phony generation."[4] God must literally enter into us to do in us, for us, and through us what we cannot do. Always has been this way, is this way, always will be this way.

God continues in Ezekiel 36:24–29, saying He is the one who will make them clean. He must give them a new heart and put a new spirit in them—His own! God says, "And I will put my Spirit in you and move you to follow my decrees and be careful to keep my laws" (v. 27). All other versions of Scripture, including ESV, NASB, and KJV, use the word *cause* instead of *move*, as used in the NIV. In other words, here is the New Covenant of the Spirit: "And I will put my Spirit in you and [cause] you to follow my decrees and be careful to keep my laws." Again in 37:14, "I will put my Spirit in you and you will live"—that is, "You will be alive spiritually, following my decrees and being careful to keep my laws." We come alive spiritually when we are born of the Spirit (John 3:3–8). Before that, we are spiritually dead (Ephesians 2:1–5) and incapable of doing anything righteous before God.

– 2 –

God's New Way

2 CORINTHIANS 3:4–6

For the Lord bestows his blessings there,
where He finds the vessels empty.
—Thomas à Kempis

Let's look together at the words of the apostle Paul in 2 Corinthians: "Such confidence as this is ours through Christ before God. Not that we are competent in ourselves to claim anything for ourselves, but our competence comes from God. He has made us competent as ministers of a new covenant—not of the letter but of the Spirit; for the letter kills, but the Spirit gives life" (2 Corinthians 3:4–6).

To fully understand Paul and his ministry, it is crucial that we see him as preacher, teacher, and excited herald of the New Covenant of the Spirit.

Paul describes himself and his fellow workers as ministers of a New Covenant of the Spirit. This new covenant is not like the old covenant of the letter of the law. The law kills. That is, because of the sinful nature that lives in us, the law inevitably brings forth failure and sin, which in turn causes separation from God, which is death. The Spirit gives life. The Spirit gives life "in order that the righteous requirements of the law might be fully met in us, who do not live according to the sinful nature but according to the Spirit" (Romans 8:4).

The righteous requirements of the law are fully met *in* us, not *by* us. These requirements are fully met in us by the Holy Spirit living in us and through us. This is because as true, reborn Christians, we no longer live controlled by the sinful nature, but we live controlled by the Spirit of God living in us.

> *The Holy Spirit cannot come to live inside a person without genuine, significant change.*

A few sentences later, Paul says to the believers at Rome, "You, however, are controlled not by the sinful nature but by the Spirit, if the Spirit of God lives in you. And if anyone does not have the Spirit of Christ, he does not belong to Christ" (Romans 8:9). As Christians, we need to be hearing about and talking about the control of the Holy Spirit in our lives much more than is currently happening. We cannot rejoice and rest in something we don't know about.

As Christians, we have received the Holy Spirit. He lives in us, in the core of our being. He is the firstfruits. He is the deposit guaranteeing the rest of our inheritance (Ephesians 1:13–14). Of course, all Christians have all of the Spirit indwelling them. It is at the level and to the degree that He gains control of every facet of us that His influence and control are experienced by us. We must become "spiritual" Christians instead of "natural" persons or "fleshly" Christians (1 Corinthians 2:14–3:3).

To some extent, every truly reborn Christian is going to be different than he or she was before rebirth and different than the world. It must be this way for the simple fact that the Holy Spirit of God has literally come to live inside of us. The Holy Spirit cannot come to live inside of a person without there being some degree of genuine, significant change. (See 1 John 3:9–10.)

Remember what I shared with you in the Introduction concerning my own conversion—how, when I woke up the next morning after having prayed to receive Christ the night before, I felt clean within and caring toward others. I wanted to help people and even wanted to share the Truth I had found. And I did help people, and I did begin enthusiastically telling friends what I had found and even saw some results. Two close friends believed in Jesus shortly after me, mainly because of the changes they saw in me and my life. It wasn't until later when I learned that witnessing, among other things, was what I was *supposed* to be doing, that I began to inwardly struggle and lose my joy. There was also further inward struggle, some loss of joy, and depression that began a few weeks after my conversion because of some pretty intense spiritual warfare and God's beginning His work in me of unpacking old baggage.

Sanctification is real. Being transformed by the renewing of our mind, our deep inner mind, being conformed to the likeness of His Son, being transformed into His likeness with ever-increasing glory, is a lifelong process performed by this same Holy Spirit living inside of us. Sanctification is the process by which God causes us to let go of control at ever-deepening levels of our being. It is the process by which God frees us more and more from ourselves and gives us more and more of Himself experientially because He chooses to. It is the process of His filling us up more and more, as we let go of control more and more, at deeper and deeper levels of our being.

Where God finds space created by brokenness, He enters. Where God finds space created by our letting go of control, He enters. In other words, the Holy Spirit living inside of us always fills up in us those spaces created by brokenness. He fills those spaces with Himself.

As Thomas à Kempis said, "For the Lord bestows his blessings there, where He finds the vessels empty."[1] By *empty*, à Kempis

11

means empty of self and self-will as opposed to God's will. "Yet not what I will, but what You will" (Mark 14:36).

By *brokenness* we mean brokenness of our own self-will in opposition to God's will, either knowingly or unknowingly. Brokenness = being caused by God to let go of control at whatever level within us we are insisting upon that control and inwardly fighting to keep it, either knowingly or unknowingly. This explains much, if not all, of our inward struggles as Christians. It is a struggle for control. (See Galatians 5:16–18.)

Also, the level at and the degree to which we are experiencing the control and filling of the Holy Spirit in our lives is a matter of faith. Faith comes from hearing the message, and the message is heard through the word of Christ (Romans 10:17). We are not hearing the message of the New Covenant of the Spirit enough. It is not being taught enough from the pulpit or in the Sunday school class and small group. Because this message of living by the Spirit is so contrary to the subtle, prideful voices of our sinful nature and the world, we must hear the message over and over again. The repetition you will encounter while reading these pages is intentional, by design and born out of this writer's excitement about the truth he is sharing and his ardent desire for you, the reader, to "get it" and/or to be encouraged in it at the level and to the degree you already do get it.

Because I am "reason[ing] with [you] from the Scriptures, explaining and proving" (Acts 17:2–3) the full meaning of the New Covenant of the Spirit, there is some repetition as I show how so many different passages teach and explain the same truth and implications of our oneness with Christ.

Live by the Spirit

Regarding what I said above about Christians not hearing enough the message of the New Covenant of the Spirit, let's look briefly at Galatians 5:16: "So I say, live by the Spirit, and you will not gratify the desires of the sinful nature."

I believe we spend too much time focusing on and preaching and teaching about the negativity of sin, how to manage it, and how we should be living. It seems to me, according to this verse, that if we spent more time and effort focusing on and preaching and teaching about what it means to live by the Spirit, the church would be sinning

> *Living by the Spirit through faith is the key to everything.*

less and would be much further along in being a testimony of Christ's reality to the world around us. With an emphasis in our teaching and preaching on living by the Spirit, the church would be sinning less and the nations would be much further along in knowing that God is the Lord because He would be showing Himself *holy* through us before their eyes (Ezekiel 36:23)

John Piper said, "God is not looking for people to work for Him but people who let Him work mightily in and through them."[2] Notice, we must be willing to let God work mightily *in* us in order for Him to work mightily *through* us. We'll be looking more deeply into what this means in part 4, "Sanctification and the Role of Suffering."

Paul says that the righteous requirements of the law are fully met in us, who do not live according to the sinful nature but according to the Spirit (Romans 8:4). So as the church comes to better understand what it means to live according to the Spirit, as taught in Galatians 5:16 and Romans 8:4, Christ's body here on earth will be sinning less and keeping God's moral law more. And, again, back to Ezekiel 36:27 and the New Covenant: "And I will put my Spirit in you and [cause] you to follow my decrees and be careful to keep my laws."

So we see that living by the Spirit through faith is the key to everything. It is the only way God reveals Himself to the world as He really is. This is what the world needs to see and know: God showing Himself holy through us before their eyes. God Himself must do it through us.

The church is no more capable of doing this than were the Israelites. Along with ancient Israel, when we have followed our own reasoning and wisdom and leaned on our own understanding, the church of Jesus Christ has done its share of profaning His holy name among the nations.

We need a better understanding of the New Covenant of the Spirit that Paul teaches. We need a better understanding and a deeper experience of living by the Spirit. We need to be whole people before the eyes of a watching world. No matter how sincere or well intentioned our efforts may be, the world sees through all pretension. Our Christianity must be who and what we are when we're just being who and what we are while Christ is living in us. Our faith must be who and what we are when we're just living in His Spirit. The world, our children, and everyone else will see through anything else. To be honest, I myself have little interest in being around Christians who are acting Christian. Give me an honest sinner any day. No wonder Jesus enjoyed eating and drinking with the tax gatherers and sinners. He probably found them refreshing.

Jeanne Guyon wrote, "If godliness is not from deep within you, it is only a mask."[3] I would say it this way: If godliness is not who and what you are when you're just being who and what you are, it is only a mask.

At what level and to what degree is Paul saying to each of us, "Are you so foolish? After beginning with the Spirit, are you now trying to attain your goal by human effort?" (Galatians 3:3). This is a very inward thing and each of us must be brutally honest with ourselves and with God regarding this question.

A Call to Teachers and Leaders

There is something else we must see in Paul's words in 2 Corinthians 3:4–11 and Romans 7:4–6. (Please read these passages at this point.) In 2 Corinthians 3:6 Paul says, "He has made us competent as ministers of a new covenant—not of the letter but of the Spirit; for the letter kills, but the Spirit gives life."

Those who have been called to be "ministers," those of us who have been called to teach and preach the Word of God, those of us who are pastors and elders, have been called to be ministers of a new covenant—a New Covenant of the Spirit. And God has made us competent to be so. Those of us who have been called to teach and preach have been called to know and understand and teach and preach the New Covenant of the Spirit.

Or will we say along with Nicodemus, "How can this be?" And then will Jesus have to say to us, "You are Israel's teacher, and do you not understand these things?" (John 3:9–10). Is He saying this now? Or even, when we come before Him at the last day, "You [were] Israel's teacher, and [did] you not understand these things?" We don't want this.

"For we must all appear before the judgment seat of Christ, that each one may receive what is due him for the things done while in the body, whether good or bad" (2 Corinthians 5:10).

"Not many of you should presume to be teachers, my brothers, because you know that we who teach will be judged more strictly" (James 3:1).

It is crucial that pastors and elders and Sunday school teachers teach and model the New Covenant of the Spirit to those under their care.

– 3 –

How Can This Be?

ROMANS 8:4

*The New Covenant was given to make it possible for me to
live with God as my deepest desire.*

—Larry Crabb

What does Paul mean in Romans 8:4? How and why can Paul say that the righteous requirements of the law are fully met in us who do not live according to the sinful nature but according to the Spirit? The way to understand this truth is this: Jesus, when questioned about which was the greatest commandment in the law, said, " 'Love the Lord your God with all your heart and with all your soul and with all your mind. This is the first and greatest commandment. And the second is like it: 'Love your neighbor as yourself.' All the Law and the Prophets hang on these two commandments" (Matthew 22:37–40).

Paul tells us in Romans 13:8–10, "Let no debt remain outstanding, except the continuing debt to love one another, for he who loves his fellowman has fulfilled the law. The commandments, 'Do not commit adultery,' 'Do not murder,' 'Do not steal,' 'Do not covet,' and whatever other commandment there may be, are summed up in this one rule: 'Love your neighbor as yourself." Love does no harm to its neighbor. Therefore love is the fulfillment of the law."

The fruit of the Spirit is love (Galatians 5:22). Love is the fulfillment of the law. Therefore, the righteous requirements of the law are fulfilled in us who do not live according to the sinful nature but according to the Spirit. As we are controlled by the Spirit, we will love God with all our heart, soul, mind, and

> *Are you content with a lifestyle of fail and confess?*

strength, and we will love our neighbor as ourselves. Living by the Spirit is the only way we will keep the law and obey God's commandments (Ezekiel 36:27). Again, it is therefore crucial that we come to understand and walk in the truth and freedom of the New Covenant of the Spirit if we are to glorify God before the eyes of a watching world.

> I run in the path of your commands, for you have set my heart free. (Psalm 119:32)

The only way we will run in the path of God's commands is if we have had the experience of having our heart set free. Free from what? Free from sin (see John 8:31–38), free from the law, and "free indeed" (John 8:36). It is the freedom to just live and be myself and, as I do so, to bear the fruit of righteousness naturally and as the norm. All for the same reason: coming to "know the truth" (John 8:32) of the New Covenant of the Spirit.

Do you believe you can love the Lord your God with all your heart and with all your soul and with all your mind? Do you believe you can love your neighbor as yourself? God gives His commandments with the expectation that His people obey them.

Do good to your servant, and I will live; I will obey your word. (Psalm 119:17)

How will the psalmist obey God's Word? The psalmist will obey God's Word by God first doing good to him so that he lives. Not just any good, but a good that causes the psalmist to live in accordance with God's law. Living and obeying God's Word are equated in this verse. The good that God does to us that causes us to live in accordance with God's Word is the New Covenant of the Spirit.

And I will put my Spirit in you and [cause] you to follow my decrees and be careful to keep my laws. (Ezekiel 36:27)

I will put my Spirit in you and you will live. (Ezekiel 37:14)

The only way we live is by God putting His Spirit in us. Living = obeying God's Word. Therefore, the only way we obey God's Word is by Him putting His Spirit in us.

Are you content with not obeying God's Word? Are you content with not fully keeping His commandments? Are you content with a lifestyle of fail and confess . . . fail and confess . . . fail and confess?

But, again, Paul states that the righteous requirements of the law are fully met in us (not by us) who do not live according to the sinful nature but according to the Spirit. In other words, as we are living according to the Spirit, we will be keeping God's moral law. We keep God's moral law by living according to the Spirit. So how crucial is it that Christians understand what it means to live according to the Spirit and how we do it? Shouldn't living by the Spirit be the emphasis in our teaching and preaching as it was in Paul's?

Living in Reality

> For what the law was powerless to do in that it was weakened by the sinful nature, God did by sending his own Son in the likeness of sinful man to be a sin offering. And so he condemned sin in sinful man, in order that the righteous requirements of the law might be fully met in us, who do not live according to the sinful nature but according to the Spirit.
>
> You, however, are controlled not by the sinful nature but by the Spirit, if the Spirit of God lives in you. And if anyone does not have the Spirit of Christ, he does not belong to Christ. (Romans 8:3–4, 9)

As Christians, do we expect to be sinning or do we expect not to be sinning? How each of us answers this question is crucial. How we answer this question reveals whether or not we are living in reality. Living in reality is believing what the Bible says about us. We can only be content, free, sane, and whole when we're living in reality. Growth in faith = God bringing us closer and closer to living in reality.

We can love God and love our neighbor as a lifestyle, as the norm in our life, without constant striving and effort. Are you satisfied with less than "fully" (Romans 8:4) and resigned to the belief that you're "just a sinner saved by grace" and that's as good it gets in this life? Or is it that you're just fatigued and resigned because of continual defeat and failure? (See Matthew 11:28–30.)

Surely "fully" in Romans 8:4 must include the most fundamental aspects of the law regarding loving God with our whole heart, soul, mind, and strength, and loving our neighbor as ourselves. How then is this possible? Paul says it's by living "according to the Spirit." Because love is the fulfillment of the law, and the fruit of the Spirit is love (Galatians 5:22), so as we are being controlled by the Spirit by faith, we will be loving God and loving our neighbor as a lifestyle, not sinning as a lifestyle. And we will be fulfilling the law or, as Paul says, the righteous requirements of the law will be fulfilled in us as we simply live according to the Spirit by faith. In this sense, living in the Spirit by faith is just living, because we already are controlled by the Spirit (Romans 8:9).

The Holy Spirit makes possible for us what it is impossible by us.

Living by the Spirit is not something additional we do as Christians; it is something we believe about ourselves because it is already true about us. In other words, we count on the fact that Romans 8:4 and 9 are true about us, and therefore we just live. Letting go of self-effort and striving at whatever level you're doing this and choosing to just live is the proper faith response to Romans 8:4 and 9.

"Be still, and know that I am God" (Psalm 46:10). Being still = just living because we expect Him to be living through us as we do so, because this is what God says He will do. Being still, ceasing striving—this is how we come to know that He is God, not us. It is how we come to know "His work in producing reality in our experience."[1]

Living in reality allows me to just live. Reality is that I'm controlled by the Spirit now. For the Christian, to live according to the Spirit is to just live because, according to Paul, writing by the moving of the Spirit, we already are controlled by the Holy Spirit living in us (Romans 8:9). This is the crucial walk of faith we as Christians must learn if we are to be glorifying God before the nations by God Himself showing Himself holy through us (Ezekiel 36:23). We just live because we believe what Scripture says about us = living in reality.

To the Christian living by the Spirit through faith, Scripture goes from being a law or rule book to being a guideline. The focus needs to go from trying to live the Bible to living by the Spirit ... then we will be living the Bible by faith instead of by self-effort. "And I will put my Spirit in you and [cause] you to follow my decrees and be careful to keep my laws" (Ezekiel 36:27). We need to begin believing this. It is at this point that the freedom Jesus and Paul talk about will begin to make sense and become real. We will be a beautiful church in whom and through whom Christ Himself is living and working as we just live.

Larry Crabb said it this way: "The New Covenant was given to make it possible for me to live with God as my deepest desire."[2] The Holy Spirit makes possible for us what it is impossible by us. "With man this is impossible, but with God all things are possible" (Matthew 19:26). The context of this verse is about true inward change, something the rich young man cannot do for himself. In fact, it would have been easier for a camel to go through the eye of a needle than for this rich young man to meaningfully change himself. The *this* in this verse, the *this* which is impossible, is every and any inward change that is spiritually significant or meaningful. Again, Ezekiel 36:27: "And I will put my Spirit in you and [cause] you to follow my decrees and be careful to keep my laws," because this is the only way it's going to happen. This is grace He has "lavished on us with all wisdom and understanding" (Ephesians 1:8).

In his book titled *Bone of His Bone*, F. J. Huegel states,

> There is not a New Testament requirement that does not immediately bring the believer face to face with an overwhelming dilemma. Either he must cease to move in the realm of the purely natural—die to the "flesh-life" and find in the resurrected Christ a new life—or he must fail as a Christian. To the new life—the life that flows from Christ—the Sermon on the Mount presents no problems.[3]

– 4 –

We Already Have It, We Just Need to Know It

1 CORINTHIANS 2:12

He who will ever cling to natural reasoning and ability in his journey to God will not become a very spiritual person.
—Attributed to St. John of the Cross

First Corinthians 2:12 assures us of this: "We have not received the spirit of the world but the Spirit who is from God, that we may understand what God has freely given us."

Much of what faith is has to do with coming to hear, realize, believe, and count upon those things that Scripture says are already true about us. Hebrews 11:1 tells us that "faith is being sure of what we hope for and certain of what we do not see." What are some of the facts that Scripture says are true about us, even though our feelings and experiences would indicate they are not true? What are some of those truths we must be certain about even though we may not "see" them in our feelings and experiences or understand them by our own reasoning?

Regarding faith, three things are true:

1. We are guilty of not having faith.
2. Only the Holy Spirit can give faith.
3. We don't need to understand this.

We dare not limit God to the confines of our limited created minds and human reasoning. However fearfully and wonderfully made we are, we are not God. We are the creature and He is the creator. We are the clay and He is the potter.

> "For my thoughts are not your thoughts, neither are your ways my ways," declares the LORD. "As the heavens are higher than the earth, so are my ways higher than your ways and my thoughts than your thoughts." (Isaiah 55:8–9)

We must each answer the question for ourselves: "If Scripture says something is true about me, and my experience and/or reason indicates it isn't true, which is true?" Obviously, Scripture must be right. There must be something else going on that's causing me to miss out on experiencing in my day-to-day life what is true about me in reality. This would have to do with lack of knowledge, and thereby unbelief, or maybe just pure unbelief. "How, then, can they call on the one they have not believed in? And how can they believe in the one of whom they have not heard? And how can they hear without someone preaching to them?" (Romans 10:14).

So, it has to do with hearing and believing. People must hear, and God must work belief in their hearts. "Consequently, faith comes from hearing the message, and the message is heard through the word of Christ" (Romans 10:17). So, in these pages, we are looking at truths that Scripture says pertain to us but that we find hard to believe because of our feelings and experiences, or, in other words, because of unbelief. Or maybe because we just haven't heard them before or enough.

Larry Crabb describes unbelief this way: Unbelief: "He (God) can't be *that* good!" → (leading to) Independence from God/Dependence on Self."[1] This is a good understanding of unbelief to be mindful of and refer back to as we read and think about some of these scripture passages. Unbelief begins with the inner thought, "He can't be *that* good!"—or in other words, "That's too much grace!" Or even, "That's

> *We dare not limit God to the confines of our limited created minds and human reasoning.*

being irresponsible. *I* have to do *something*." Our response to this thought is subtle, inward movement toward independence from God and dependence on self, leading to sin, increasing frustration, and inevitable failure. (See Romans 7:14–25.)

As F. J. Huegel wrote in *Bone of His Bone*, "But this victory is achieved only through death, for the 'self-life' and the satanic spirit are in unconscious affinity."[2]

Sanctification is the process by which those things that are true about us factually are becoming more and more true about us experientially. By grace through faith over time, what is true about us factually becomes more and more real in our experience. Along with the psalmist, we can say about God's sanctification process, "the LORD has done this, and it is marvelous in our eyes" (Psalm 118:23).

Also, "He who did not spare his own Son, but gave him up for us all—how will he not also, along with him, graciously give us all things?" (Romans 8:32). What things? Greater and greater experiential knowledge of, understanding of, believing in, and thereby resting in those things that are already factually true about us. To quote the Puritan theologian John Owen: "Resting in Him as [my] utmost end."[3] Or, as I would put it, " 'Just living because He's living through me' as my utmost end."

"We have not received the spirit of the world but the Spirit who is from God, that we may understand what God has freely given us" (1 Corinthians 2:12).

It is only by hearing, understanding, heart-knowing, believing, and thereby resting in the truth of the New Covenant of the Spirit that the glorious freedom we actually, factually have as God's children becomes real in our experience. My prayer is that you'll "see" and believe as you read these two volumes concerning the New Covenant of the Spirit.

Faith is a strange thing. I think the year was 1971. I was hitchhiking back up to Syracuse University after a weekend visit home on Long Island. It was raining out on Route 17. I was about a year old in the Lord and, of course, I was praying for a ride. After a while, a small four-seater foreign car containing three hippies pulled over for me. Just as they stopped, the car conked out. As I got in, the Holy Spirit showed me in my mind all that was about to happen. I knew the car wasn't going to start, that I was going to pray, the car was going to start after I prayed, and I was going to witness about Jesus to these guys.

Sure enough, the driver turned the key, and we listened to the final, slow-motion death moans of a motor at the mercy of a dead battery. The driver tried again . . . death. The hippies were morose. But, as I said, I knew what was going to happen. I said, "Everyone just wait a minute." To this day I wish I had prayed out loud. I put my head down and asked the Lord to show Himself to these guys. I lifted my head. "Try it now." *Vrooom* . . . it started right up. The hippies were happy.

"Oh, hey, man, far out . . . how'd you do that, man?" Another one said, "It's like the power of the mind, man!" I quickly replied, "No, no, no . . . it was Jesus. I prayed and asked Him to start the car." Silence. "Let me read something to you." I handed out three copies of *The Four Spiritual Laws* booklet, and I read it to them cover to cover as we drove down the highway. After I finished, there was silence for the rest of the ride. I think I shared some of my own testimony. More silence. When their route veered from mine, we pulled over and I got out. We said our goodbyes and I continued hitchhiking up to Syracuse, rejoicing.

Jesus lives through us and gives adventures as we're available. I don't know if the three guys ever believed. I do hope to see one or two, or maybe all three, in heaven.

A few weeks later, my Campus Crusade for Christ group and I were at a retreat. When it was time to go home, someone's car wouldn't start. "No problem," I said. "Gather 'round." We all held hands around the car and I prayed, this time out loud. Nothing happened. Oh well, so much for my burgeoning car-healing ministry. Like I said, faith is a strange thing.

"Our God is in heaven; he does whatever pleases him" (Psalm 115:3).

– PART 2 –

Freedom

– 5 –

Running in the Path
of His Commands

PSALM 119:32, 45

*We can learn nothing of the gospel, except by feeling its
truths. . . . There are some sciences that may be learned by the
head, but the science of Christ crucified can only be learned
by the heart.*

—Charles Spurgeon

Psalm 119:32, 45 tells us this: "I run in the path of your commands, for you have set my heart free . . . I will walk about in freedom, for I have sought out your precepts."

It is only in knowing and experiencing freedom from the law that I'll find myself joyfully running in the path of it. We run in the path of His commands only as we just live and find ourselves keeping His commands because we are being filled up and led by the Holy Spirit. (See also Ephesians 5:17–20; Ezekiel 36:27.)

The apostle Paul, in the New Testament book of Galatians, assures us of this: "But if you are led by the Spirit, you are not under law" (Galatians 5:18).

We will only find ourselves running in the path of His commands at the level and to the degree we have had our heart set free. We will only find ourselves running in the path of His commands at the level and to the degree we are experiencing freedom from the law and the joy that comes with this freedom in our Christian life. We will only find ourselves running in the path of His commands at the level and to the degree we have had our heart set free due to coming to know the reality of consistently living under the real, loving control of the indwelling Holy Spirit. We will only run in the path of His commands at the level and to the degree we know freedom, the freedom to just live and to see ourselves running in the path of those commands at the same time because of the Spirit's control in our life (Romans 8:4, 9). We will only be running in the path of His commands at the level and to the degree that we are being controlled by the indwelling Holy Spirit (Galatians 5:16, 22–23). We will only be running in the path of His commands at the level and to the degree we are being caused to by God Himself living in us (Ezekiel 36:26–27; Romans 8:9).

I run in the path of Your commands because it's no longer up to me to keep them.

When we understand this teaching of freedom in the Spirit, we can say to the Lord: I run in the path of Your commands because it's no longer up to me to keep them. I couldn't run in the path of them if I tried (Romans 7:14–25). I run in the path of Your commands because You Yourself, living in me, cause me to keep them as I just live (Ezekiel 36:27). I run in the path of Your commands because I love them, because You Yourself, living in me, give me the desire to keep them and the joy that comes from seeing them fulfilled in me and through me as I just live (Ezekiel 36:26; Philippians 2:13; Romans 8:4). I run in the path of Your commands because I am no longer yoked to them. I run in the path of Your commands because it's no longer up to me to keep them, but rather I find myself keeping them as I just live (Romans 8:4).

This is freedom "indeed" (John 8:36). This is "just living." This is wholeness.

Wholeness is being free to just live while being godly at the same time, as I'm just living, because of Jesus living in me, filling me and living through me. Believe it or not, this is where God is bringing us. This is the "free indeed" that Jesus is talking about in John 8:36. This life-changing truth must and will be felt and *known* inwardly. Only Christians can be whole persons. It is something God has for us now, in this life. It is known experientially by grace through faith, like everything else in the Christian life.

Just Living

The freedom to just live is experienced only by those who believe Christ will be living through them as they do so. Do you see the connection here? Believing Christ will be filling me and living through me is what frees me and allows me to just live = wholeness. This is what Paul means by living by the Spirit through faith. This is the truth that sets us free (John 8:32). This is Jesus's teaching of the Vine and branches in John 15. *This* is where God is bringing us.

Also, I choose just living (= abiding) over self-effort because I believe Jesus when He says that abiding (= just living) is how I will bear much fruit (John 15:5). I want to bear much fruit, instead of just some fruit, because this is how my Father is glorified (John 15:8). I believe that Jesus Himself, living through me, can do it better than I can "with His help." The only truly free Christians are those who have come to the place of believing that Jesus is and will be living through them as they just live. The only truly free Christians are those who believe that Jesus Himself is causing and moving them from within to will and to act according to His good purpose (Philippians 2:13). In other words, the only truly free Christians are those who have come to know and understand that it is no longer they who live but Christ who lives in them (Galatians 2:20), and that He will be working in them to will and to act according to His good purpose as they simply live their lives.

The seventeenth-century French believer Jeanne Guyon wrote, "Great faith produces great abandonment."[1] In other words, great faith produces great "just living." The old spiritual word *abandonment* (to God) is synonymous with the spiritual term *just living.* You will only understand these words in your spirit because it is "spiritual truth" (1 Corinthians 2:13). Trust God to enable you to begin to "feel" (Spurgeon) these truths as we continue.

We will be most obedient as we are most abandoned to God. This is because it is true that Jesus lives through us as we just live (Romans 8:9). I will be most obedient and fruitful when I am most abandoned, because it is true that all I am is a branch. A unique, one-of-a-kind, beautiful, beloved, special, gloriously created branch, but just a branch nonetheless. Everything comes from the Vine through me (read Ezekiel 36:23 again) as I just live. (For further study, John 15:5 is Jesus's commentary on Ezekiel 36:23, and John 15:5 interprets and explains Ezekiel 36:23.)

As Christians, if we are really going to make a difference among the nations and in the towns and neighborhoods where we live, we must come to this place of believing that Jesus will be living through us as we just live, and that He Himself will do a better job through me than I will do through self-effort "with His help." Jesus doesn't want to help us; He wants to live His life through us. He said, "I am the vine; you are the branches" (John 15:5). I believe that Jesus is and will be living through me when I'm just living = abiding.

Andrew Murray wrote, "[Humility is] the nothingness that makes room for God to prove His power."[2] In other words, humility is the "just living" that makes room for God to prove His power by filling me and living through me as I do so. (See also Psalm 46:10.)

> *"The cross . . . always has its way"; God always wins, because His love is unfailing.*

God brought me to the place of just living over a period of years. I learned obedience from what I suffered. The freedom I was aware of in my spirit and wanted more than anything, my sinful nature resisted and fought against just as hard (Galatians 5:16–18). The inward battle for control was often intense and all-consuming. For a variety of reasons, knowing this freedom to just live doesn't come easy, but it is worth everything I had to go through to attain it. "The cross . . . always has its way"; God always wins, because His love is unfailing.[3]

For me, as it is or will be for many of you, just living is a freedom from overthinking, compulsive thinking, having to be in control, and leaning on my own understanding. It is freedom from the slavery of too much introspection and "self-interested turning inward upon myself" (Fénelon). It is freedom from self-willed "reflective operations" (John of the Cross). It is the freedom of living by the Spirit (spirit) instead of by the head. It is freedom from the all-too-common problem of Christian enslavement to a "perpetual struggle of the head." It is freedom from the rampant sin of insistence on control, the misery that comes with it, and the foolishness that thinks you have or need some control.

Instead of continually looking inward, and thereby being virtually unavailable to others, I am now free to look outward as I go through my day and be available to people in friendly and refreshing ways, as Christ Himself fills and lives through me. It is just living in the moment, moment by moment, because of confidence in the fact that Jesus is and will be filling and living through me, because He said He would. It is finally letting go of too much thinking, striving, and fleshly self-effort in all its insidious forms at all its insidious levels. It is also called *wholeness*, and it is where God is bringing us.

Perfect Passivity with the Highest Activity

Let's consider something else Andrew Murray said: "The soul in which the wondrous combination of perfect passivity with the highest activity is most completely realized, has the deepest experience of what the Christian life is."[4]

What is Murray saying here? How can one have inward "perfect passivity" and great inward and outward activity at the same time? This is possible because it is true that Jesus lives through us as we just live. "Perfect passivity" = just living, because it is true that God works in you now, not the sinful nature, to will and to act according to His good purpose. He reigns in you now, not the sin nature. (See Philippians 2:13; Romans 6 and the diagram on p. 49; and Romans 8:9.)

How are John 15:5; Romans 8:4, 9; Galatians 5:16–18; Ephesians 5:18–20; and Philippians 2:13 saying anything different from what God is saying in Ezekiel 36:26–27? All of these scriptures are speaking of the same thing: the New Covenant of the Spirit. If the New Covenant of the Spirit is true, can't you just live? Can't you just live and find yourself being more fruitful than ever before at the same time—that is, experiencing "perfect passivity with the highest activity"? Do you see how believing this = great freedom, freedom "indeed," freedom to just live (John 8:36)? The Christian life is Jesus living through you as you just live. The one thing needed (Luke 10:42) is Jesus Himself. The one thing needed is receiving from Jesus, like a branch receives from a vine. The one thing needed is the risen Word of God (John 1:1–2) living in you and through you as you just live. This is "what God has freely given us" (1 Corinthians 2:12).

This will be difficult for some of us. There is an inner struggle going on. The whole passivity/activity thing creates emotion in us. We will look at the underlying centuries-old passive/active issue in more detail soon. Believe it or not, there is a simple answer.

Knowing God's Truth Results in Freedom

Seeking out God's precepts will bring us to the place of walking about in freedom (Psalm 119:45). Diligent seeking out of God's precepts will inevitably bring us to this place of freedom (John 8:32, 36; John 16:12–13; Psalm 25:14; Matthew 7:7–8; Romans 8:31–32). This is because, in diligently seeking out God's precepts, the Holy Spirit will lead us to the place of understanding the New Covenant of the Spirit. The precept we need to know in order to walk around in freedom is the New Covenant of the Spirit.

"The LORD confides in those who fear him; he makes his covenant known to them" (Psalm 25:14). The covenant He makes known to us is the New Covenant of the Spirit.

Please notice that the psalmist in 119:45 has simply experienced what Jesus says will happen in John 8:32. The end result of seeking out God's precepts is walking in freedom. Jesus is saying the exact same thing when He asserts that if we hold to His teaching, as we continue to follow Him and learn from Him, we will know the truth and the truth will set us free. True knowledge of Jesus results in freedom, freedom from sin as a way of life, freedom from the law, and freedom "indeed," the freedom to just live and be myself. As I do so, I will experience righteousness and bear much fruit, and this will be the norm for my life. The truth we come to know, that sets us free as we continue in Jesus's teaching, is the New Covenant of the Spirit. "So I say, live by the Spirit, and you will not gratify the desires of the sinful nature" (Galatians 5:16). This verse is the "truth" Jesus is talking about in John 8:31–36. Seeking out God's precepts results in knowing freedom. The more you come to know His precepts, the more you come to know freedom.

This book is intended to help you come to know freedom and the joy that comes with it. It is intended to help you come to the place of wholeness = just living and finding yourself being good and loving at the same time, just living and finding yourself being Christlike at the same time. Wholeness, or just living, is where the Holy Spirit is bringing us. It is good and helpful to know where we are headed, as far as possible. It is good and helpful to know God's purposes and will for us, and to some degree, how He is bringing us there.

Julian of Norwich, an English anchoress in the Middle Ages, said this: "If God wishes to show you more, he will be your light; you need none but him."[5]

Her words reflect the teaching of the apostle John when he wrote, "But when he, the Spirit of truth, comes, he will guide you into all truth" (John 16:13).

It is good to understand this truth that God is faithfully, continually working in us, in His perfect timing, in His perfect way, to free us from ourselves and bring us to the place of greater and greater experiential freedom, wholeness, authenticity, and holiness as we just live, because He chooses to. As we shall see later, all of our inward struggles and battles are interpreted and explained by God's Word, are interpreted and explained by God working in us to free us from ourselves and to give us Himself (Galatians 5:16–18).

It is good to have our heart set free by coming to know that we can just live, as we actually begin to believe that we are no longer controlled by the sinful nature but by the Holy Spirit who lives in us. When I actually begin believing that I'm now controlled by the Holy Spirit who lives in me, I become free to just live. I become free to just be who I am. I become a whole person.

The church and the world desperately need Christians who are whole persons. Whole persons are Christians who know the reality of being able to just live and be themselves because they know the reality of the indwelling Christ controlling them and living through them. This is where God is bringing us. God's bringing us there explains the inward struggling we go through.

The fact is that as Christians, we're free to just live because we're controlled by the Holy Spirit. This is wholeness. This is the good news of the New Covenant of the Spirit. It is how we powerfully change the world around us, by just living = living by the Spirit = wholeness and Christlikeness because He lives through us as we just live, like a branch in a Vine.

This freedom and wholeness and Christlikeness, all at the same time, culminate in God's promise to us in the New Covenant, the New Covenant of the Spirit, as He states in Ezekiel 36:26–27. Read again this passage and Romans 8:4, 9 and please see the connection. Romans 8:9 is simply Paul's affirmation of God's promise to His people, to His church, both Jew and Gentile, in Ezekiel 36:26–27. Begin understanding Paul as the excited herald of the New Covenant, the New Covenant of the Spirit. Oh, that we would become likewise.

− 6 −

Free Indeed

JOHN 8:31–36

*In almost everything that touches our everyday life on earth,
God is pleased when we're pleased. He wills that we be as free
as birds to soar and sing our maker's praise without anxiety.*
—Attributed to A. W. Tozer

What does it mean that we are "free indeed"? To answer this question, let's first look at the teaching of Jesus in John 8:

> To the Jews who had believed him, Jesus said, "If you hold to my teaching, you are really my disciples. Then you will know the truth, and the truth will set you free."
>
> They answered him, "We are Abraham's descendants and have never been slaves of anyone. How can you say that we shall be set free?"
>
> Jesus replied, "I tell you the truth, everyone who sins is a slave to sin. Now a slave has no permanent place in the family, but a son belongs to it forever. So if the Son sets you free, you will be free indeed." (John 8:31–36)

To the Jews who had believed Him, not necessarily who "put their faith in him" as the "many" in verse 30, Jesus says that if they hold or continue in His teaching, then they are really His disciples, and then they will come to know the truth and the truth will set them free. The Greek word for *know* in verse 32 means a deep experiential relational knowing, a heart knowing, versus a mere head knowledge of facts. It is the kind of knowing that changes a person. Knowing the truth that Jesus is speaking of has the effect

> *Wholeness is the freedom to just live, and to be Christlike as we do so, because Jesus is living through us.*

of setting disciples of Christ free. French mathematician and Christian thinker Blaise Pascal put it this way: "The heart has its reasons, which reason does not know."[1]

What is this truth that will set disciples free? What does it set disciples free from? We see in verse 36 that it is the Son, it is Jesus, who does this work of setting free. We see from the context that Jesus is speaking of freedom from sin. He is speaking of freedom from slavery to sin. In other words, Jesus is speaking of freedom from the controlling power of sin over the sinner, from the mastery of sin in his or her life (John 8:34–36).

Jesus is referring to three related freedoms: freedom from sin as a way of life, freedom from the law, and freedom to just live and be ourselves. As we live in this freedom, righteousness and fruit will be the norm instead of sin and failure. This is what Jesus means by being "free indeed." This is "free indeed" freedom. Jesus is giving His hearers, and readers, a glimpse of what "wholeness" is and where it comes from. Wholeness is where God is bringing His disciples, those who continue in His teaching. Wholeness is where God is bringing us. Wholeness is the freedom to just live, and to be Christlike as we do so, because Jesus is living through us. This is the Sabbath rest that still remains for the people of God (Hebrews 4:9–10).

Imagine the wonderful freedom of being able to just live and be ourselves and not be sinning at the same time! Imagine the wonderful freedom of being able to just live and be ourselves, with righteousness and fruit being the norm at the same time! This is "indeed" freedom . . . this is wholeness. This is one of those glorious gifts that God has "freely given us" (1 Corinthians 2:12) and that the Holy Spirit enables us to understand as we hold to and continue in Jesus's teaching (John 8:31). It is truth that sets us free. It is where God is bringing us. It is where God is bringing us so that we can change the world around us as He shows Himself holy through us as we just live.

This is the New Covenant of the Spirit as promised by God in Ezekiel 36:26–27: "I will remove from you your heart of stone and give you a heart of flesh. And I will put my Spirit in you and [cause] you to follow my decrees and be careful to keep my laws." We have all this because of and through Jesus Christ.

The truth that Jesus is referring to in John 8 is this: If Christ is in me and He's controlling me, then I'm free. I'm free from sin as a way of life, I'm free from the law, and I'm "free indeed." I'm free to just live and be myself and experience righteousness and fruit as the norm instead of failure and sin. This is good news! This is grace. This is the New Covenant of the Spirit. Freedom is because of union.

– PART 3 –

Union

– 7 –

Channels Only

JOHN 15:1–5

*Abiding in Jesus is not a work that needs each moment
the mind to be engaged, or the affections to be directly
and actively occupied with it. It is an entrusting of oneself
to the keeping of the Eternal Love, in the faith that it
will abide near us, and with its holy presence watch over
us and ward off the evil, even when we have to be most
intently occupied with other things. And so the heart has
rest and peace and joy in the consciousness of being kept
when it cannot keep itself.*

—Andrew Murray

As I shared in the Introduction, I was converted in October 1970 as a freshman at Syracuse University in upstate New York. A couple of guys from Campus Crusade for Christ (known now as CRU) shared the gospel with me in my dorm room. A few nights later I prayed and surrendered my life to Christ. I was cleansed and born of the Spirit that night.

In 1970 the Jesus Movement was at its height in our nation. It was a remarkable revival and work of the Holy Spirit that began on the West Coast and was spreading eastward. I remember reading articles about it in *Life* magazine and seeing the photos shortly after my conversion. I was quite blown away. Most of the converts were hippies and surfers and street people who had come to Jesus. It was a true work of the Holy Spirit and a delight to be part of.

> *A branch has no will of its own. It has no life of its own. The vine is its life.*

A few weeks after my conversion, my best friend "Kenny" likewise became born again. He couldn't deny the radical change he saw in me and prayed to receive Christ. That following summer Kenny and I decided to fly out to California to see what was going on firsthand. We ended up at a Baptist Church just off Pacific Beach in San Diego. We stayed in a school bus converted into sleeping quarters in the back parking lot of the church building for about three days.

On Wednesday evening, the church was having their "Wednesday 7" meeting. Kenny and I went in. There were about a hundred hippies and surfers, all carrying Bibles, mostly sitting cross-legged on the floor of the fellowship hall. After a little while, a quiet, middle-aged man came out and introduced himself as the pastor. He began his lesson. It was from John 15:1–5, Jesus's teaching about the Vine and branches:

> I am the true vine, and my Father is the gardener. He cuts off every branch in me that bears no fruit, while every branch that does bear fruit he prunes so that it will be even more fruitful. You are already clean because of the word I have spoken to you. Remain in me, and I will remain in you. No branch can bear fruit by itself; it must remain in the vine. Neither can you bear fruit unless you remain in me. I am the vine; you are the branches. If a man remains in me and

I in him, he will bear much fruit; apart from me you can do nothing. (John 15:1–5)

The pastor had a bunch of grapes from the local grocery store in his hand. He taught us the following:

"We don't have a whole grapevine here, so the bunch of grapes will suffice. The main stalk is Jesus, and the crooked little branches that are attached to the 'vine' (stalk) are us, the true Christians. Now the grapes are out on the ends of the branches so it looks like the branches made the grapes. But the grapes are the fruit of the vine. As the branches just remain, just abide, just live attached to the vine, the life-giving sap, the Holy Spirit, flows from the vine and out through the branches, and the grapes come out on the end of the branches. You will never see a branch straining and striving and suddenly a grape pops out. No, but as the branch just abides, just lives in its oneness with the vine, the fruit comes out naturally and without effort on the part of the branch. Jesus is the Vine; you are just branches. As you just remain in Jesus, He will be living through you, and you will bear much fruit to the glory of the Father. What fruit? The fruit of the Spirit, which is love, joy, peace, patience, kindness, goodness, faithfulness, gentleness, and self-control, as well as seeing others come to Jesus through you."

I've never forgotten this teaching. I have learned to utterly count upon it. It has "set me free"; it has set me free to just live (John 8:32, 36; Psalm 119:45), and it does so for you as well.

A branch has no will of its own. It has no life of its own. The vine is its life. (See Colossians 3:1–4). Everything is oneness with the vine ... the branch's life is one with the vine's life. A branch just lives with the life of the vine flowing through it. Everything is oneness with the vine, including the pruning. (More on "pruning" when we look at "Sanctification and the Role of Suffering.")

– 8 –

He Reigns in You Now, So Just Live

EZEKIEL 36:26–27 AND PHILIPPIANS 2:12–13

*I must learn that the purpose of my life belongs to God, not
me. God is using me from His great personal perspective, and
all He asks of me is that I trust Him. . . . When I stop telling
God what I want, He can freely work His will in me without
any hindrance.*

—Oswald Chambers

When we read Ezekiel 36:27 and Philippians 2:12–13, we
see that these three verses, one from the Old Testament
and two from the New Testament, are saying the same thing. That
same thing is the "New Covenant of the Spirit" (2 Corinthians
3:6).

> And I will put my Spirit in you and move (cause) you to
> follow my decrees and be careful to keep my laws.
>
> (Ezekiel 36:27)

> Therefore, my dear friends, as you have always obeyed—not
> only in my presence, but now much more in my absence—
> continue to work out your salvation with fear and trembling,

46

for it is God who works in you to will and to act according to his good purpose. (Philippians 2:12–13)

Both passages are declaring the truth that when we put our faith in Christ, God's Spirit lives in us and will be causing and moving us to follow His decrees and keep His laws as we just live. It is God Himself who works in us now, not the sin nature, to will and to act according to His good pleasure. The Greek word for "works" in the Philippians verse is *energeo*, which means "to be operative, be at work, put forth power." God moves in us and we obey that moving. The Christian life is simply obeying the controlling, reigning, ruling Holy Spirit. And He *will* be reigning in us as we just live. The Bible says so. These two scriptures, along with many others, say so.

The Holy Spirit in us is the normal voice now as we just live. (See the Romans 6 diagram on page 49.) His is not the loudest voice, but His is the deepest. His is the fundamental voice, the central voice, the normal voice in us now. His is the normal voice as we just live.

The normal, easiest, most trouble-free life for a slave (Romans 6:17–19) is to simply yield to and obey the master's voice.

> *It is God who rules in your heart now, so you are free to just live.*

According to Paul, we have a new master now which is the Holy Spirit in us. Our master is no longer the sin nature. We are free to just live and find ourselves being obedient at the same time, for it is God who works in us—this is the norm now, not the sin nature working in us like it was before we believed—to will and to act according to His good purpose. It is in believing this truth that we will become free (John 8:32).

In John 10:27, Jesus said, "My sheep listen to my voice; I know them, and they follow me." It is interesting that Jesus does not say, "My sheep listen to my voice; they know me, and they follow me." The reason Jesus says "I know them" at this point is because He is saying, "Because I know my sheep intimately (after all, I created each one's inmost being and knit each of them together in their mother's womb), I know how to speak to each of them in a way that they can hear me. I call each of them by name, and they follow me."

Continue to just live, continue to work out the salvation you already have, continue getting up in the morning, going to work, doing the hard things God has for you to do, living your life, making hard choices and decisions, by the Spirit putting to death the misdeeds of the body, continuing to just live in the midst of fearful and challenging situations.

Consider Paul's teaching on sin and freedom in Romans 6:17–19:

> But thanks be to God that, though you used to be slaves to sin, you wholeheartedly obeyed the form of teaching to which you were entrusted. You have been set free from sin and have become slaves to righteousness. I put this in human terms because you are weak in your natural selves. Just as you used to offer the parts of your body in slavery to impurity and to ever-increasing wickedness, so now offer them in slavery to righteousness leading to holiness.

Continue just living your life with confidence, because it is God living in you and controlling you now (Romans 8:9), not the sinful nature. It is God working in you now to will and to act according to His good purpose, not the sinful nature. It is God who rules in your heart now, so you are free to just live. He is the normal voice in you now, so just live = wholeness = where God is bringing us by grace through faith. The New Covenant of the

Spirit is the truth that sets us free. You can do as the psalmist: "I will walk about in freedom, for I have sought out your precepts" (Psalm 119:45).

I'm free because I'm controlled by the Spirit living and ruling in me = Ezekiel 36:26–27 = the New Covenant of the Spirit.

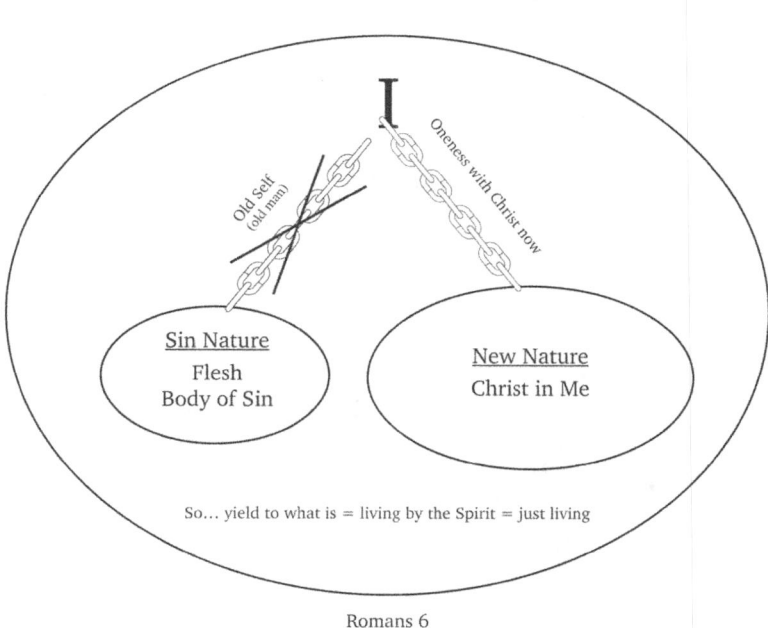

Romans 6

– PART 4 –

Sanctification and the Role of Suffering

– 9 –

Gracious Affliction

PSALM 119:67–72, 75

Where brokenness is invited and received with grace,
the gospel comes alive with hope.

—Larry Crabb

Donna and I own a vacation/retreat house in the Pocono Mountains in northeast Pennsylvania. We spend family vacations there, and we sometimes enjoy going up during the winter months to get out of the city and do some writing and resting in the peace and quiet. In the evenings, we often have a fire going in the living room fireplace. We sit quietly and watch the fire. The logs do their share of shape-shifting and spark-spitting as if complaining while gradually disappearing. Or are they disappearing? Maybe what's really happening is a transformation, a beautiful and fortunate metamorphosis.

In the late sixteenth century, a Carmelite monk and poet, John of the Cross, wrote a treatise titled *Living Flame of Love*. In his poem of the same name, he refers to God Himself as the Living Flame of Love. Sitting in front of his own fireplace one evening, he observed how the log, while being consumed by the fire, was itself becoming a warmth-giving, light-giving flame. In its own disappearance as a dead log, it was becoming one with the living flame. The log itself was being transformed into flame.

The thoughtful monk goes on to compare this natural transformation to Christian sanctification. Kind of lends a whole new meaning to and perspective on the fact of our God being a "consuming fire," doesn't it? (Deuteronomy 4:24; Hebrews 12:29). Indeed, our God is the Living Flame of Love. In dying inwardly to self-will and control, in yielding to God's loving, continual working in us to surrender more deeply to Him, we gradually become more and more experientially one with the Living Flame of Love. A flame is ongoing and continual, as is God in His working in us to conform us to the likeness of His Son. Flame is painful. This is His love that surpasses knowledge (Ephesians 3:19; Job 7:19).

All affliction, great and small, comes from God and is for our good and His glory.

Andrew Murray said, "The only sure mark of the presence of God [is] the disappearance of self."[1]

The author of Psalm 119 knew about affliction. The psalmist confesses that affliction was the instrument God used to cause him to become obedient:

> Before I was afflicted I went astray, but now I obey your word.
> You are good, and what you do is good; teach me your decrees.
> Though the arrogant have smeared me with lies, I keep your precepts with all my heart.
> Their hearts are callous and unfeeling, but I delight in your law.
> It was good for me to be afflicted so that I might learn your decrees.

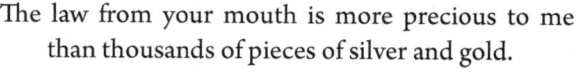

The law from your mouth is more precious to me
than thousands of pieces of silver and gold.

. . . .

I know, O LORD, that your laws are righteous, and in
faithfulness you have afflicted me.

(Psalm 119:67–72, 75)

God afflicted the psalmist as discipline for both willful and indwelling sin. The affliction came as persecution in the form of ridicule and false accusation from the arrogant around him. Affliction changed his heart by causing him to humble himself before God and submit to His word. The psalmist confesses that affliction in his life was an act of God's goodness toward him. It was instrumental in bringing the psalmist to a place of delighting in God's law. The psalmist is glad he was afflicted because he sees that affliction is how he came to learn God's decrees inwardly and deeply.

God used the discipline of affliction to change the psalmist's heart, to further sanctify him. (See Hebrews 12:7.) And, of course, He does so with us. It is part of His love that surpasses knowledge. (See also Job 7:17–19.) God either causes or permits everything that comes into our lives. Therefore, all affliction, great and small, comes from God and is for our good and His glory.

As with the Psalmist, So with Us

We must be broken inwardly if we are to come to a place of delighting in and learning God's law and decrees. We must be broken of indwelling sin in the form of self-will and pride. Only God can bring us to a place of genuinely loving His law.

The terms *God's law*, *decrees*, and *precepts* are all terms having to do with God's covenant requirements. In keeping God's commandments as Christians, the covenant we are under is the New Covenant of the Spirit. We serve in the new way of the

Spirit versus the old way of the written code (Romans 7:6). The requirements and terms of this New Covenant are spelled out in Jeremiah 31:31–34 and Ezekiel 36:26–27. Please reread these passages at this time.

Therefore, our part in this covenant is to simply humbly receive from God, like a branch receives from the vine. Our part in this covenant is to be the blessed receiver of all God says He will be doing in us, for us, and through us. We are brought to the humbling place of "I can't" in order to be brought to the blessed place of "I don't." He *is* our life now (Colossians 3:4).

Andrew Murray said, "All Christ's teaching of His disciples, and all their vain efforts, were the needful preparation for His entering into them in divine power, to give and be in them what He had taught them to desire."[2]

It is in knowing that it is not up to us to keep the law, but that God Himself wills to be keeping it in us and through us as we just live (Romans 8:4), that we can begin to love the law and delight in it. At the level and to the degree that we still believe that part of keeping the law is up to us is at the level and to the degree that we will not be genuinely delighting in it and enjoying keeping it. The only way we will begin to love the law and delight in it, never mind start keeping it, is when we come to the place of experiencing Jesus Himself living in us and keeping it through us as we just live. As we just live, the Holy Spirit will be filling us and causing us to love and obey God and to love and serve those around us. The more freedom we experience from the law while still keeping the law, the more we love the law. We love the law because we're no longer *under* it but find ourselves naturally keeping it as we just live.

"I run in the path of your commands, for you have set my heart free" (Psalm 119:32). I run in the path of Your commands, for You have set my heart free from being "under" them, for You have set my heart free from being the one who has to keep them. I run in the path of Your commands because You fill me and live through me as I just live. You have said You will do this and You will!

We genuinely delight in God's law and enjoy keeping it only when we see ourselves keeping it as a result of being filled up, controlled by, moved and caused to keep it by the indwelling, controlling Holy Spirit. It is only in knowing freedom from God's law that we begin to genuinely love it. It is only as we experience ourselves being righteous, keeping the law, and bearing fruit naturally as we just live that we will find ourselves delighting in the law. It is only in no longer being under the law that we can begin to love the law (Psalm 119:32, 45). Until we come to know that we are nothing but receivers, we will not be able to genuinely echo the psalmist in Psalm 119. It is only in knowing grace and truth fully that we can genuinely rejoice and delight in God and His commandments.

As we mentioned earlier, F. J. Huegel wrote,

> There is not a New Testament requirement that does not immediately bring the believer face to face with an overwhelming dilemma. Either he must cease to move in the realm of the purely natural—die to the "flesh-life" and find in the resurrected Christ a new life—or he must fail as a Christian. To the new life—the life that flows from Christ— the Sermon on the Mount presents no problems.[3]

Like the psalmist, it takes being afflicted for us to finally come to the place of learning, agreeing with, and submitting to the absolute surrender terms of the New Covenant of the Spirit. We must lose the battle for control (Galatians 5:16–18). Anything less than dying to self, anything less than total surrender, is prideful and misdirected, no matter how well-intentioned. The response to His mercy that God is interested in and desires is offering our body a living sacrifice. This is our reasonable service of worship. The essence of worship is surrender.

What Must We Do?

Beware of the disastrous "Well, *you* have to do something" way of thinking. What does a branch do? Go and do likewise. Because of oneness with the Vine, what you have to do is just live. And even that is only by grace through faith and because Jesus lives in you and is moving and causing you to do so. You no longer live, but He lives in you. He *is* your life = He *is* your *everything* in you and for you (John 15:5; Galatians 2:20; Colossians 3:1–4). The response to His mercy that interests God is faith and absolute surrender.

> Then they asked him, "What must we do to do the works God requires?" Jesus answered, "The work of God is this: to believe in the one he has sent." (John 6:28–29)

To believe in the One He has sent for everything. To believe in Jesus for forgiveness and eternal life and to believe in Jesus for sanctification and living the Christian life—to believe in Jesus living in us and through us for everything, like a branch connected to a vine. A branch connected to a vine just lives. This is why Jesus said that believing in Him is the whole work that God requires, because the Christian life is Him living in us and through us as we just live. So, abiding in Him, abiding in the Vine, just living, is all we must do to accomplish the works God requires, the works God predetermined for each of us to do.

> For we are God's workmanship, created in Christ Jesus to do good works, which God prepared in advance for us to do.
> (Ephesians 2:10)

To believe in the One He has sent is all the "work" God requires because of the New Covenant of the Spirit. To believe in Jesus is the whole work that God requires because the Christian life, following God's decrees and being careful to keep His laws, fully happens by Jesus living His life in us and through us. This is also why the "one thing needed" is receiving from Jesus . . . the one thing needed is Jesus Himself (Luke 10:42).

> *If you no longer live, what is it exactly that you can depend upon yourself for?*

In saying these things, I am not describing radical Christian living. We are talking about normal Christian living. The indwelling Christ filling and living through us as we just live is not radical Christian living; it is normal, scriptural Christian living. It is how God has always meant it to be. It is not the "deeper life"; it is normal life, it is the Christian life, and it's for all believers.

Knowing God's Precepts Results in Freedom

We must have our hearts set free by knowledge of the New Covenant of the Spirit before we will find ourselves running in the path of His commands. The Psalm 119 psalmist genuinely loved God and His commandments because he had come to know heart-level freedom through studying and learning God's precepts.

> I will walk about in freedom, for I have sought out your precepts. (Psalm 119:45)

Serious, humble study of God's precepts, of His Word, results in coming to know freedom. The more one truly knows Scripture, the more one knows freedom. We must have our heart set free at whatever level and however subtly we still believe that we ourselves must do something in this business of living the Christian life. That thinking is prideful self-delusion. It is at the level and to the degree that we believe this and think this way that we will not be delighting in God and His law. We will only be delighting in God's law at the level and to the degree that we come to know that it's not up to us to keep it—that we no longer live, but He lives in us (Galatians 2:20; Romans 8:4). That the life you now live in the body you live by faith in the Son of God, who loves you and gave Himself for you.

If you no longer live, what is it exactly that you can depend upon yourself for? What is it exactly that one can depend upon a dead person for? Since you no longer live, you must rely upon Him living in you for everything. You must believe that you no longer live, but He lives in you, and so you live accordingly, like a branch in a Vine, which is just living = freedom.

What Exactly Is "Dying to Self"?

Fénelon said, "Whatever light, whatever feeling we may possess, is all a delusion, if it lead us not to the real and constant practice of dying to self."[4] This, to me, is the meaning of his words: Dying to self = just living.

Dying to self is dying to self-effort, to self-absorption under the pretense of correcting our faults, and to self-absorption in the form of compulsive thinking and introspection in order to get a feeling of control. The opposite of these things is just living because of a confidence in the fact that Jesus living in you is and will be controlling and living through you as you just live = living according to the Spirit = the New Covenant of the Spirit = Romans 8:4, 6, 9.

Dying to self = letting go of control at ever-deepening levels of our being. Dying to self = letting go to Christ's will and control = freedom. If Christ is in me and He's controlling me, then I'm free, free to just live. I will walk about in freedom, for I have sought out His precepts. Seeking out God's precepts results in walking about in freedom. It is freedom from the world, the worldly, the sinful nature, and the devil. Regarding freedom from self, experiential freedom from the sinful nature, Fénelon wrote, "You are also inside us . . . in that inaccessible church and sanctuary of our souls. . . . It is there that are put to death all of our selfish desires, all of our self-interested turning inward upon ourselves, and all of our movements of self-love."[5]

The above quote accurately interprets and explains 99.9% of your inward struggle, if not all of it. (See Galatians 5:16–18.) There are deep-rooted, sin-nature-based "selfish desires," patterns of "self-interested turning inward," and "movements of self-love" going on within you that God the Father, Son, and Holy Spirit must put to death. This is hard to go through, but it is worth it. It is sin that lives in us (Romans 7:17, 20) that God is freeing us from = sanctification.

Jean-Pierre de Caussade summarizes it this way: "Is it not, on the contrary, this resistance [(to letting go), this struggle (for control)], which we too often continued without owning it even to ourselves which is the cause of all our troubles?"[6]

It's All About God Giving Us Himself in Ways We Don't Understand

Dying to self is an inward thing. Dying to self = just living. Just living because I believe the Scriptures that Jesus lives in me and is and will be filling and controlling me as I just live = having my heart set free and walking about in freedom because I have come to "see" and believe this precept of the New Covenant of the Spirit. I run in the path of His commands because I have had my heart set free by Jesus Himself coming to live in my heart and filling me and controlling me and causing me to follow His decrees and keep His laws. So I'm free . . . free from sin as a way of life, free from the law, and free "indeed," free to just live and be myself and find myself running in the path of His commands at the same time. All for the same reason . . . if Jesus lives in me and He's controlling me, I'm free = John 8:32, 36 = the New Covenant of the Spirit = wholeness = where God is bringing us by grace through faith.

– 10 –

What Paul Wants

PHILIPPIANS 3:10–11

*Religious experience for Paul is basically
experience of union with Christ.*
—J. D. G. Dunn

L isten to the words of the apostle Paul in Philippians 3:10–11:
"I want to know Christ and the power of his resurrection and
the fellowship of sharing in his sufferings, becoming like him in
his death, and so, somehow, to attain to the resurrection from the
dead."

Paul's deepest, most heartfelt desire is to know Christ. By this,
Paul means to know Christ personally, intimately, relationally,
and experientially = to *know* Him and to relate with Him from
his "gut," to relate with Him from his innermost being. He wants
to know Him so intimately as to become one with Him, in union
with Him. More than anything, Paul desires experiential oneness
with Christ. Paul wants to lose himself in Christ, for "it is by losing
myself in You that I become one with You."[1]

Another way of saying the same thing is "For it is by just
living that I become one with You." Christians who live their
lives counting solely upon their actual vital union with Christ for
everything are going to change the world around them. They will
bear "much fruit" and "fruit that remains."

Paul wants to know the "power of His resurrection." To know the power of His resurrection is to know the power that comes from experiential oneness with Him now, in this life, while living in this world. We are one with Him already. Paul is saying what he wants more than anything is to know this oneness in his experience, in his day by day, moment by moment experience. He already has been raised with Christ. He is in Christ and Christ is in him. For him, to live *is* Christ. He wants the implications and results of this actual oneness to be real in his life. There is no one more powerful than someone through whom Christ Himself is free to live, unhindered by stubborn overactivity and vain striving after righteousness.

Paul wants to know Christ and the "fellowship of sharing in His sufferings." Why would Paul ever want to know this? Why would Paul ever want experiential oneness with Christ to go that far? Because he knows that this is a crucial component of coming to know his Lord experientially/relationally, and knowing Jesus experientially/relationally and bringing others to that same knowledge is all that Paul cares about. He knows that knowing Christ really is the best thing there is. He knows that knowing Christ intimately/relationally is heaven on earth.

Paul would shudder at the thought of not knowing Christ, of somehow missing out because, at some level of his being, he refused to do and experience whatever it takes to know Him. Paul knows that sharing in the fellowship of the Suffering Servant's sufferings, that sharing in the fellowship, both inwardly and outwardly, of the experiences of the "man of sorrows, familiar with suffering" (Isaiah 53:3) is a crucial factor in coming to know Him. Wanting to know Christ far outweighed any fear or shying away from suffering, even though that fear and temptation to shy away from it was there. (See 1 Corinthians 2:1–5.) Paul knew deep within himself that suffering was one of the crucial components in how one comes to know great experiential oneness with the risen Christ Jesus in this life.

Larry Crabb puts it this way: "I have come to believe that suffering is necessary to awaken our desire for God and to develop confidence in His desire for us."[2]

Intimacy with Christ Really Is the Best Thing

Because of the Spirit's working in him, and only because of that, Paul was loving God with all his heart and with all his soul and with all his mind in his willingness and sincere desire to participate with Jesus in the fellowship of sharing in His sufferings and becoming like Him in His death so as to know Him better. Paul knew that offering his body as a living sacrifice in light of God's mercies (Romans 12:1) really was the best thing and the only way he was going to come to "know Christ." Paul was willing to go through whatever it took to know Christ. The Spirit can and does and will work this willingness and desire in us as well.

The apostle states that the fitting response to knowing the fellowship of sharing in Christ's sufferings, that the fitting response to suffering, is "becoming like him in his death" (Philippians 3:10). What does he mean here?

Paul's passion and ardent desire is to be like Christ, to have Christ living through him freely and unhindered. He knows he has been predestined to be conformed to Christ's likeness (Romans 8:29) and Paul is all for it, no matter what it takes. He knows he can do and endure all things through Christ who strengthens him (Philippians 4:13). By this he means he knows he can do and endure all things because of oneness with Christ, because of Christ living in him, because of Christ living in him who is his strength (Psalm 73:26; Colossians 3:4).

Attaining to the Resurrection from the Dead?

There is an effective, necessary, subtle progression in Philippians 3:10–11 that must happen within us to attain to "the resurrection from the dead." Before we answer the question of what it means to become like Christ in His death, we need to understand what Paul means by attaining to the resurrection from the dead.

Paul already had the resurrection from the dead. He was saved. Having believed, he was marked in Christ with a seal, the promised Holy Spirit, who was a deposit guaranteeing Paul's inheritance (Ephesians 1:13–14). He knew the Lord would rescue him from every evil attack and would bring him safely to His heavenly kingdom (2 Timothy 4:18). The resurrection from the dead was certainly not something Paul had to attain or could have "attained to," in the sense of earning it or living up to it, in order to be sure he had it. Paul had already attained the resurrection from the dead by grace through faith, as all true believers have.

> *We must become like Him in His death to be like Him in His life.*

To attain to the resurrection from the dead is to advance spiritually to the place where one's experience and behavior match what he or she already has and is in Christ. In verses that follow, Paul calls this being made "perfect." Another word for perfect is *complete* or *whole*. Attaining to the resurrection from the dead, or being made "perfect," is when our actual, factual, already possessed oneness with Christ becomes more and more real in our experience. To attain to the resurrection from the dead is to attain to experiential oneness with Christ, in character and behavior and power, by grace through faith.

How Does Actual Oneness Become Experiential Oneness?

We are already raised up with Christ (Ephesians 2:4–7; Colossians 3:1–4). We died with Christ, and we have been raised up with Christ. We are in Him and He is in us, like a branch joined to a Vine. We are one with the Vine. How does this oneness become true in our experience? How do we come to know, experientially, the power of His resurrection which we already partake of and participate in actually?

Paul prays for the Christians at Ephesus:

> That you may know the hope to which he has called you, the riches of his glorious inheritance in the saints, and his incomparably great power for us who believe. That power is like the working of his mighty strength, which he exerted in Christ when he raised him from the dead and seated him at his right hand in the heavenly realms, far above all rule and authority, power and dominion. (Ephesians 1:18–21)

Going back to Philippians 3:10–11, Paul is saying that how we come to know Christ intimately, relationally, and experientially, and how we come to thereby know the power of His resurrection—that is, how we come to know oneness with Him experientially—is by knowing the fellowship of sharing in His sufferings and, in response to this suffering, becoming like Him in His death. Oneness with Christ experientially involves knowing Him and being like Him in terms of His character and knowing Him and being like Him in terms of His power to live life here on earth as He lived it. This all happens by knowing the fellowship of sharing in His sufferings and becoming like Him in His death.

Jesus says in John 14:12, "I tell you the truth, anyone who has faith in me will do what I have been doing. He will do even greater things than these, because I am going to the Father."

When He says "because I am going to the Father," He means that He will be sending the Advocate, the Holy Spirit, to dwell with us and in us here on earth (John 16:7).

We must become like Him in His death to be like Him in His life. This is what Paul recognized, and this is what Paul is teaching. It is through dying that we live = it is through dying that we become one with Christ experientially = it is through dying that Christ lives His life through us because of unhindered oneness, like a branch in a Vine. This dying is a dying to self. This dying is a letting go of self and self-will at deeper and deeper levels of our being so that Christ may more and more live through us unhindered.

We Long for Perfection = Completeness = Experiential Oneness = Wholeness = Rest

Notice that Paul says *somehow*: "and so, somehow, to attain to the resurrection from the dead" (Philippians 3:11). There's a mystery to it. Somehow, through the fellowship of sharing in Christ's sufferings and, in response, becoming like Him in His death, is how we come to more and more actualize and realize oneness with Christ . . . in this life, here on earth. Somehow, through the fellowship of sharing in His sufferings and, in response, becoming like Him in His death, we come to experience oneness with Christ in terms of being like Him in character and behavior and power and thereby become powerfully effective in influencing and changing the people and situations around us, like Jesus was and like Jesus did.

To attain to the resurrection from the dead is to become, in our character and behavior, who and what we already are in actuality and reality = one with Christ. This comes about through the fellowship of sharing in His sufferings and, in response to this suffering, becoming like Him in His death.

To attain to the resurrection from the dead is to be made "perfect" (Philippians 3:12). Not that we can attain to this perfection, not that we can attain perfect experiential oneness with Christ in character and behavior and power in this life, but we press on. We can advance in this experiential oneness with Christ in this life a whole lot more than we think by participating in the fellowship of sharing in His sufferings and becoming like Him in His death.

Paul was not satisfied with anything less than being made perfect. Paul was not satisfied with anything less than greater and greater experiential oneness with Christ = knowing Christ. "I want to know Christ" = "I want oneness with Christ" = "I want oneness with Christ experientially, relationally, and behaviorally." According to Paul, this oneness with Christ experientially/relationally/spiritually is comparable to a man and a woman becoming one flesh physically/relationally/spiritually. More on this shortly.

Paul was willing to go through whatever it took to "gain Christ," to gain this experiential oneness with Him, and he did go through what it took . . . the fellowship of sharing in Christ's sufferings, becoming like Him in His death. When Paul met Christ on the road to Damascus, he was blinded and rendered helpless. God sent a man named Ananias to Paul to pray for him, so that his eyes might be opened. When Ananias, knowing Paul as a persecutor of the church, hesitated to respond to God's call, the Lord said to him, "Go! This man is my chosen instrument to carry my name before the Gentiles and their kings and before the people of Israel. I will show him how much he must suffer for my name" (Acts 9:15–16).

Earlier in the book of Philippians, after giving a long list of his worldly accomplishments and accolades, Paul writes:

> But whatever was to my profit I now consider loss for the sake of Christ. What is more, I consider everything a loss compared to the surpassing greatness of knowing Christ Jesus my Lord, for whose sake I have lost all things. I consider them rubbish, that I may gain Christ and be found in him, not having a righteousness of my own that comes

from the law, but that which is through faith in Christ—the righteousness that comes from God and is by faith.

(Philippians 3:7–9)

To summarize so far, Paul is writing about what he wants more than anything—knowing Christ = experiential oneness with Christ in this life = gaining Christ = attaining to the resurrection from the dead. Attaining to the resurrection from the dead = experiential oneness with Christ in this life. Paul also describes how he will get this = knowing (experientially and relationally) the fellowship of sharing in Christ's sufferings and, in response to this suffering, becoming like Him in His death. Life, for Paul, is experience of union with Christ. God has this for each of us as well. It is where He is bringing us.

Knowing Christ Is Oneness with Christ

In Scripture, including Paul's use of the word here, to "know" and to "become one with" are synonymous. In the English Standard Version of the Bible (ESV), Genesis 4:1 reads, "Now Adam knew Eve his wife, and she conceived and bore Cain, saying, 'I have gotten a man with the help of the LORD.'" (See also Genesis 4:17, 25.)

In Ephesians 5:31–32, Paul writes, "'For this reason a man will leave his father and mother and be united to his wife, and the two will become one flesh.' This is a profound mystery—but I am talking about Christ and the church."

Marriage between a man and woman is meant to be a picture and example to the world around us of Christ's relationship with the church, with you and me. We are the bride of Christ. A husband is to love his wife as Christ loved the church and gave Himself up for her, and a wife is to respect her husband; she is to submit to him as the church submits to Christ.

The "profound mystery" is that, somehow, this becoming one flesh between a husband and wife that takes place through a physical act is similar and comparable to our oneness with Christ that takes place spiritually through participation with Him in His death and resurrection (see Romans 6 and the diagram on page 49). It is a deep, real, spiritual union of love, peace, joy, fruitfulness, and suffering that can be known experientially as we just live. This is how Paul wants to more and more know Christ.

Before we get into Philippians 3:12–14, let me make a detour to another passage that stresses the primacy of knowing Christ and experiential oneness with Him in living the Christian life.

John 17:20–23, 26

Think deeply about Jesus's prayer for us as you read . . .

> My prayer is not for them alone. I pray also for those who will believe in me through their message, that all of them may be one, Father, just as you are in me and I am in you. May they also be in us so that the world may believe that you have sent me. I have given them the glory that you gave me, that they may be one as we are one: I in them and you in me. May they be brought to complete unity to let the world know that you sent me and have loved them even as you have loved me. . . . I have made you known to them, and will continue to make you known in order that the love you have for me may be in them and that I myself may be in them.
> (John 17:20–23, 26)

Jesus makes it clear that the way in which the world is going to believe that the Father has sent the Son is through oneness. First, we would be one with the Father and the Son. Just as the Father is in Jesus and Jesus is in the Father, Jesus prays that we would be in the Father and Son so that the world may believe that the Father has sent Jesus. Jesus explicitly says in verses 21–23 that the way the world is going to believe that the Father has sent the Son is by our being in the Father and the Son, and by the Father and the Son being in us. Of course, these oneness terms imply oneness of wills—being yielded to the Spirit and controlled by Him.

Second, what is implied is not only positionally being one with the Father and the Son but experientially, as this oneness is made evident to the world by the fruit we bear as a result of this oneness, like a branch and a vine. In the same discourse with His disciples, just before this prayer, Jesus has stated that He is the Vine and they are the branches. It is by our counting upon this oneness with the Father and the Son as we just live (= abiding) that Jesus lives through us unhindered and makes Himself evident to the world around us by our bearing the fruit of the Spirit, by our "good life, by deeds done in the humility that comes from wisdom" (James 3:13). We just live because we believe that Jesus Himself lives in us and will be living through us as we do so, because He said He would.

This is what it means "to abide." We do so because we believe that our oneness with the Son and the Father is real. "Abiding" or "remaining" = just living = living by the Spirit through faith = Galatians 2:20 = the "exchanged life." Living by the Spirit is normal Christian living. We live in unity with the one who loved us and gave Himself for us. This is the "first love" to which the church at Ephesus needed to return (Revelation 2:4–6).

We would do well to pay close attention to Jesus's exhortation in Revelation 2:1–7. The degree to which the Ephesian church members had left their first love was the degree to which they had left the Holy Spirit, in their individual lives and thereby as a church. Their doctrine was great; their spirits were not. We must hear Jesus's warning and tremble.

Jesus's prayer in John 17:20–26 has been answered; reborn Christians are one with the Father and the Son. We just need to know it. We just need to know its implications better and believe it more. If and when we do, in that moment we will come to know the freedom of the "exchanged life" and "just living."

Be Still and Know That I Am God, Not You

Jean-Pierre de Caussade, in *Abandonment to Divine Providence*, wrote, "You seek perfection, and it is in everything that presents itself to you. Your sufferings, your actions, your attractions are the species under which God gives Himself to you, while you are vainly striving after sublime ideas."[3]

Our oneness with the Father and the Son needs to become more real in our experience. Our oneness with the Father and the Son needs to become more visible in our lives so that the world can respond to it, one way or the other. This happens by faith and the fellowship of sharing in His sufferings and, in response to those sufferings, becoming like Him in His death so that He can live through us unhindered by our "vainly striving after sublime ideas."

> Be still, and know that I am God; I *will* be exalted among the nations, I *will* be exalted in the earth. (Psalm 46:10, emphasis mine)

Let me offer you my paraphrase of Psalm 46:10. I believe this is what our Father is saying to us in this verse: "Being still is how you are going to come to know, experientially and relationally, that I am real and that I really do live inside of you and that I really can and will live through you, if you give me the chance. I will exalt myself through you among the nations as you just live and trust me; I will be exalted in the earth right where you live, as you just live and trust me to live through you, because I want people to see me and know me for who I am far more than you do. And the New Covenant of the Spirit—my filling you and living through you as you just live—is my way of doing this. Remember, as the heavens are higher than the earth, so are my ways higher than your ways and my thoughts than your thoughts, no matter how well intentioned your ways and thoughts are."

How We Reach the World, According to Jesus

It is in knowing and thoroughly counting upon, now, in this life, our oneness with the Father and the Son, and thereby experiencing this oneness more and more—that is, Jesus living in and through us—that the world is going to believe that Jesus is the Son of God. This is the only way. First, each Christian must know and thoroughly count upon his or her oneness with the Father and the Son, like a branch in a Vine, in order for the world to believe (John 17:20–21). So we must be teaching this truth.

As each Christian utterly depends upon his or her oneness with the Father and the Son, and only that, we will bear fruit. And part of that fruit, as Jesus is living through us unhindered, will be love for and oneness with each other, a supernatural oneness in the body of Christ. As the world sees us loving each other as the Father loves the Son, because of this love being in us and Jesus Himself being in us and reigning there, the world will know that Christianity is real. The world around us will either love us and come to Christ or hate us and reject our message, and maybe kill us. As Jesus is living through us, the world around us will treat us as they treated Him when He walked this earth (John 15:18–21).

Christians' experiential oneness with the indwelling Christ is the only way the world can and will be converted. To the degree the world does not see Christians loving one another and dwelling together in unity is the degree to which they will not believe that the Father sent the Son (John 17:20–23). This dwelling together in unity is only accomplished as each Christian knows and counts upon his or her oneness with Christ and the

Father for everything, including and especially our oneness with each other. Only Jesus Himself—filling us, controlling us, and living through us—brings love and unity in His body. "But the fruit of the Spirit is love" (Galatians 5:22).

So again, what should the focus and emphasis in our teaching and preaching be? What does the church today really need more than anything? What do we need to be hearing more than anything, over and over again? What does the world around us need to be seeing more than anything in order for them to believe that the Father sent the Son? According to Jesus in His priestly prayer of John 17:20–26, they need to see Christians exhibiting and proving their oneness with the Father and the Son by their loving oneness with each other. According to Jesus, experiential oneness with the Father and the Son resulting in genuine loving oneness with each other is how those who are called to be saved will be saved.

What Do We "Press On" In?

Now let's return to Paul's words in Philippians 3:10–14. How does Paul attain to the resurrection from the dead more and more in this life? How does the oneness that he already has with Christ become more and more real in his experience? How does the fact that he is dead to sin but alive to God in Christ Jesus (Romans 6:11) become more and more real in His experience? He says it is through the fellowship of sharing in His sufferings and, in response to these sufferings, becoming like Him in His death. Next, Paul clarifies . . .

> Not that I have already obtained all this, or have already been made perfect [complete, whole, Christlike in his experience], but I press on to take hold of that for which Christ Jesus took hold of me [knowing Christ and the power

of His resurrection and attainment to the resurrection from the dead as much as possible in this life]. Brothers, I do not consider myself yet to have taken hold of it [= attainment to the resurrection from the dead = perfect experiential oneness with Christ in this life = perfection]. But one thing I do: Forgetting what is behind and straining toward what is ahead, I press on toward the goal to win the prize for which God has called me heavenward in Christ Jesus.

(Philippians 3:12–14)

Paul wants to win. He wants to be the best. He wants to be the most Christlike Christian by the time he is called home.

What does Paul "press on" in or with in order to "take hold of" (make real for himself) that for which Christ Jesus took hold of him = knowing Him and knowing "perfection" = knowing Him and knowing experiential union with Him in this life = attaining to the resurrection from the dead? He presses on in wanting to know Christ and the power of His resurrection and the fellowship of sharing in His sufferings and, in response to the sufferings, becoming like Him in His death. This is what Paul presses on in so that, somehow, he may attain to the resurrection from the dead . . . so that through the fellowship of sharing in Christ's sufferings and, in response, becoming like Him in His death, he may come as close as is possible in this life to knowing perfect experiential oneness with Christ. That he may come as close as possible in this life to knowing this perfect, restful, blissful, fruitful union with Jesus "so that now as always Christ will be exalted in my body, whether by life or by death. For to me, to live is Christ and to die is gain" (Philippians 1:20–21).

Philippians 1:20–21

Jesus will be glorified in Paul's body through his union with Him. This is what Paul means. When he says, "For to me, to live

75

is Christ and to die is gain," this is not an expression of devotion or sentiment. Paul means it literally. "For to me, to live *is* Christ." It is an expression of oneness with Christ. For Paul, "For to me, to live is Christ" = "My life is Christ living His life through me." This is why Paul is so confident that "if I am to go on living in the body, this will mean fruitful labor for me" (Philippians 1:22). Paul could have added, "because my life is Christ living in me and through me as I just live . . . because I'm simply a branch in the Vine . . . because I no longer live, but Christ lives in me." Or, "Because I no longer live, but Christ lives in me, for me to live *is* Christ." Or, "For me to live is Christ, because I no longer live, but Christ lives in me."

It is a literal, actual identity statement which he went over in great detail in chapter 6 of his letter to the church at Rome. Galatians 2:20 and Romans 6 interpret and explain each other. (We will look closely at Romans 6–8 in volume 2 of this series.)

That, because of his union with Christ, because of oneness with Christ, for him to live *is* Christ and to die is gain. Because of being filled up by Christ, because of Christ literally living through him as he just lives, for him to live *is* Christ and to die is gain. This is the freeing confidence that Paul had, and it is for us to have as well (Romans 8:32).

Christ is not glorified in our bodies by our well-intentioned working for Him and our "sublime ideas." In those cases, in the eyes of those watching, we get more of the credit than Christ does. It happens all the time. We glorify men when good things happen.

Christ is glorified in our bodies by He Himself living through us as we just live. This is God's way. Well-intentioned and well-meaning but still ignorant of this truth, Christians think in terms of and talk about "living for Jesus." Disciples know better. They think and talk in terms of dying for Jesus so He can live through them. They talk about "the fellowship of sharing in his sufferings, becoming like him in his death" with the goal of Christ being exalted in their bodies, "whether by life or by death" (Philippians 3:10; 1:20).

Andrew Murray wrote, "[Humility is] the nothingness that makes room for God to prove His power."

This is Paul's passionately felt and desired goal—to know Christ, to know intimate union with Him in will, in thinking, in emotions, in attitudes, in desires, in character, in behavior, and in power so that Christ may be exalted in his body. Paul recognizes that this comes by knowing, by experiencing, the fellowship of sharing in His sufferings and, in response, becoming like Him in His death.

Knowing my oneness with Christ, and therefore just living because I'm believing that Christ will be filling and living through me as I do so, is a place of faith and understanding that only God Himself can and does bring us to, in His perfect way, in His perfect timing. We hear truth and God gives faith. That's why this book is so important and why God called and moved me to write it.

For a period of about ten years, from the early 1980s to the early 1990s, I worked under the tutelage and direction of an older Christian psychologist. He saw something in me, took me under his wing, and became a kind of spiritual father and mentor. He taught me valuable lessons and truths. He emphasized living by the Spirit and talked about an "inner confidence" we could begin to have and grow in based upon knowing and counting upon our oneness with Christ. In other words, if Christ is in me and He's filling and controlling me (Ephesians 5:18–20; Romans 8:9) as I just live, how else is He going to be leading, guiding, and directing me moment by moment, day by day, but through *me*, through my own inner thinking, judgment, and will? This is what experiential oneness with Christ *is*, and it's by faith. This was all fine and true, and I thank him for planting the seeds of knowing my identity in Christ, its implications, and how to begin living out of that identity.

But, for some reason, at some point, my mentor began to cross over from faith to presumption. It became more of an irrational "all His thoughts are my thoughts, and all my thoughts are His thoughts" kind of thing. It was a kind of unwise, inappropriate carrying of things to their logical end, a kind of overdependence on human reasoning in his application of this truth of oneness with Christ. There was no longer any room for mistakes. Every thought was automatically right and correct because it was God's thought. Needless to say, our relationship slowly dissolved as his ideas and demands became increasingly unreasonable for Donna and me. We eventually parted ways.

Faith is the highest means of knowing truth, not human reason.

All this is to say, faith is not presumption or some kind of magical thinking. We still have a sin nature that can misconstrue and twist things in our heads and emotions. In the realm of faith, we cannot always carry ideas to their so-called logical conclusion. We must be content with a degree of mystery and "darkness." We're not going to understand everything. I know it is true that I can begin having an inner confidence in my own judgment, thinking, and decisions because of oneness with Christ and the fact of His working in me to will and to act according to his good purpose. If it is true that He is living in me and leading and directing me moment by moment (Romans 8:9), how else is He going to be doing this but through *me*, through my own inner thinking, judgment, and spirit as I'm abiding (just living) in Him? Oneness with Christ does indeed imply a growing inner confidence, because it really isn't a confidence in me myself; it is a confidence in His living, moving, causing, and leading me from within me. This is a significant part of what wholeness is. But this doesn't mean that every thought I have is His. Faith is not presumption or magical thinking. We can have a growing confidence in our experiential oneness with Christ without crossing over into illusion ironically based on human logic. Faith is the highest means of knowing truth, not human reason.

"There are those learned opinions that are more fastidious than correct, more plausible than true," wrote Charles Spurgeon.[4]

We can and should have a healthy inner confidence and sense of being able to be a whole person, including a healthy trusting in my own inner person as I just live and make decisions. This is because of the truth of oneness with Christ now. We can have a healthy inner confidence because of oneness and still be living with the reality that I am capable of being wrong and sinning. I felt I needed to address the issue of faith versus presumption to some degree at this time, but this is the subject of another book.

Losers Win

Consider these words of Fénelon: "It is by losing myself in You that I become one with You."[5] We might think of it this way: Losing myself in You = just living. It is by just living that I become one with You. It is by just living that I become one with You experientially, because I already am one with You actually, factually.

The reason we become one with Christ experientially by losing ourselves in Him is because we already are one with Him actually, factually. We live in Him and He lives in us. As I let go of control at deeper and deeper levels of my being, Christ, who lives in me, fills in and fills up the open spaces with Himself. The Holy Spirit always fills the space created by letting go, created by brokenness, created by dying to self. This is because He already lives in us and "moves into" those areas of self we let go of—that is, that we die to.

Jesus told His followers in the book of John:

The hour has come for the Son of Man to be glorified. I tell you the truth, unless a kernel of wheat falls to the ground and dies, it remains only a single seed. But if it dies, it produces many seeds. The man who loves his life will lose it, while the man who hates his life in this world will keep it for eternal life. Whoever serves me must follow me [in this dying]; and where I am, my servant also will be. My Father will honor the one who serves me [by dying along with me, by becoming like me in my death]. (John 12:23–26)

Christian perfection is oneness with Christ in character and behavior and power. In other words, it is the fruit of the Spirit—love, joy, peace, patience, kindness, goodness, faithfulness, gentleness, and self-control—being who we are as we just live because we're controlled by the indwelling Holy Spirit now. It is bearing "much fruit"; it is "deeds done in the humility that comes from wisdom" (James 3:13). Christian "perfection" comes about over time by the fellowship of sharing in Christ's sufferings and becoming like Him in His death in response to these sufferings. It is the process of being conformed to the likeness of God's Son (Romans 8:29), which is God's purpose (v. 28) for every Christian, for which every Christian has been predestined (v. 29).

Every Christian has been predestined to this end, to being conformed to Christ's likeness. God's fulfilling this purpose in us interprets and explains everything we go through in this life, both outwardly and inwardly. God uses "all things" that happen to us externally and internally as contributors to His good work of conforming us to the likeness His Son. This is a major reason we are to be "always giving thanks to God the Father for everything, in the name of our Lord Jesus Christ" (Ephesians 5:20). It is the process of being made "perfect" (Philippians 3:12). Being like Christ and being "perfect" are synonymous. Being like Christ and being complete, restful, authentic, free, joyful, and whole, like Christ was and is, are synonymous.

Paul pressed on to take hold of that for which Christ Jesus took hold of him = God's "purpose" for him = to be conformed to the likeness of Christ = to know the power of His resurrection = to attain to the resurrection from the dead = experiential union with Christ. To be conformed to the likeness of Christ = experiential oneness with Christ in character and behavior and power, which comes by knowing the fellowship of sharing in His sufferings and, in response to the experience of these sufferings, becoming like Christ in His death.

What Does It Mean to Know the Fellowship of Sharing in His Sufferings?

What does Paul mean by wanting to know "the fellowship of sharing in His sufferings, becoming like Him in His death and so, somehow, to attain to the resurrection from the dead" (Philippians 3:10-11)? It is important to understand what Paul means here because it is how, "somehow," we attain to the resurrection from the dead. It is how we come to know greater and greater experiential oneness with Christ. It is how our real, actual, factual union with Christ becomes more and more real in our experience. It is how we come to actually know the experience of Christ living through us and filling us with His Spirit as we just live.

Webster's New Collegiate Dictionary defines *fellowship* as "companionship, company. A community of interest, activity, feeling, or experience." Also, "intimate personal intercourse."

The Greek word for *fellowship* in Philippians 3:10 is *koinonia*. The word means "participation, a having in common, partnership." *Koinonia* denotes "the share which one has in anything, a participation, fellowship recognized and enjoyed, thus it is used of the common experiences and interests of Christian men. In

Philippians 3:10 it is used of participation in the sufferings of Christ."[6]

So does this mean that in order to know the fellowship of sharing in our Lord's sufferings, we have to go through exactly what He did? Does it mean that, in order to participate in the sufferings of Christ, we have to also be spit upon, flogged, beaten, and crucified? Maybe we have to at least be martyred? Is it the case that, to the degree we "miss out" on these specific sufferings, we miss out on knowing Christ, knowing the power of His resurrection and attaining to the resurrection from the dead as completely as other Christians in other countries who may be being persecuted in ways that more closely match Christ's actual physical sufferings?

Let's face it; in America, at least currently, the chances of participating in Christ's sufferings in ways that match or even approach His are pretty slim. There are Christians abroad who are, but so far not Christians in our country, that I know of. Paul came pretty close, as did the other apostles and first-century Christians but not us. So what do we do? Are we doomed to mediocrity in this whole area of coming to know great, blessed, deep, and intimate experiential oneness with Christ while living in this world?

May it never be! Intimate, experiential union with our Lord in this life cannot be hindered by geography and circumstances. "He who did not spare his own Son, but gave him up for us all—how will he not also, along with him, graciously give us all things?" (Romans 8:32). This goes for all Christians, including us American silver-spoon believers.

The fact is we don't have to go through the exact physical sufferings as our Lord in order to advance just as far as any other Christian in attaining to the resurrection from the dead, in attaining to great and blessed experiential oneness and holiness with Jesus while living on this earth. All Christians have been predestined by the Father to be conformed to the likeness of His

Son, that He might be the firstborn among many brothers. The degree to which this takes place for each of us while in this life is decided upon by our Father, not by geography or circumstances. "Our God is in heaven; he does whatever pleases him" (Psalm 115:3).

The fact is we don't have to go through the same experiences outwardly in order to go through the same experiences of suffering inwardly. We don't have to go through the same experiences of Jesus outwardly in order to know the participation of sharing in His sufferings.

It Is Primarily Inward

Let's understand that sharing in Christ's sufferings is primarily an inward thing. Likewise, becoming like Him in His death is primarily an inward thing. We're just simply not all going to be in a garden, praying and sweating drops of blood, but we will have times of agonizing over felt loss of intimacy with God and abandonment by close friends. We will suffer for doing good. We will be greatly misunderstood and probably even hated and rejected by some. We don't have to be hanging on a cross to feel forsaken by God. We don't have to be hanging on a cross to be humiliated, made fun of, laughed at, and ridiculed for what we know to be true. We don't have to be praying and agonizing in a lonely garden or hanging on a wooden cross in order to feel totally alone in a world that doesn't care, in order to feel totally alone and misunderstood by a world that feasts and laughs and happily goes on with life as we suffer inwardly, unnoticed and unrecognized.

When Paul says, "I want to know Christ and the power of his resurrection and the fellowship of sharing in his sufferings, becoming like him in his death" (Philippians 3:10), he is saying, "I want to feel the same things as my Lord did; I want to know Him inwardly, experientially, relationally—this is oneness with

Him. I want to experience inwardly in my feelings and emotions and activities the power of His resurrection. I want oneness with Him inwardly in all ways so I can actually be and live like Him, so I can be Him as much as is possible while in this earthly tent. I want to become like Him in His death so I can be filled up and overtaken by Him more and more as I just live."

Dying to self, brokenness, letting go of self-will and control more and more deeply, and feeling the struggle inwardly that accompanies all this does not require going through exactly what Jesus went through outwardly. The prayer that Jesus prayed, "Yet not what I will, but what you will," is an inward thing and can be agonizingly felt and experienced without the experience of facing physical crucifixion in a few hours. "My God, my God, why have you forsaken me?" can be very really felt without hanging on a cross with the sins of the whole world on oneself.

We must recognize and take comfort in the fact that all of our sufferings and trials, outward and inward, are adequate approximations of Jesus's sufferings, allowed by the Father and qualifying as the fellowship of sharing in His sufferings. For Christians, all of our sufferings, great and small, outward and inward, are the fellowship of sharing in His sufferings. And this is a good thing. It is a good thing to know the fellowship of sharing in Christ's sufferings because it is a crucial part of coming to know Christ. And certainly, certainly, certainly, knowing Christ really is the best thing there is. It is treasure hidden in a field.

– 11 –

It's a Fellowship

HEBREWS 4:14–16

*You must learn to act calmly and in continual dependence on
the Spirit of grace, mortifying all the hidden works
of self-love.*

—François Fénelon

Just as we participate in Jesus's sufferings and temptations
while He was here on earth so that we can feel some of what
He felt and thereby know Him better, so Jesus participated in our
sufferings and temptations so that He could sympathize with our
weaknesses, so that He could feel what we feel and thereby know
us, and thereby know firsthand and experientially what it feels
like to be a human living in this world. Consider the words of
Hebrews 4:14–16:

> Therefore, since we have a great high priest who has gone
> through the heavens, Jesus the Son of God, let us hold firmly
> to the faith we profess. For we do not have a high priest who
> is unable to sympathize with our weaknesses, but we have
> one who has been tempted in every way, just as we are—yet
> was without sin. Let us then approach the throne of grace

with confidence, so that we may receive mercy and find grace to help us in our time of need.

It works both ways . . . it's a fellowship, a mutual participation. Is there any temptation that we go through as humans that Jesus didn't fully feel and can't fully relate to? According to verse 15, the answer is no. Whoever you are, Jesus knows what it feels like to be you.

He Had to Be Made like Us in Every Way

Scripture says Jesus was tempted in *every* way, just as we are—yet was without sin. Jesus knows what it feels like to be us. He knows what it feels like

> *Jesus knows what it feels like to be you.*

to be you. No matter what temptations you have gone through or go through, Jesus sympathizes with your weaknesses because He, in one form or another, felt the same things you feel. He was tempted in every way, just as you are. No one is left out, no matter what temptations and inward struggles with sin they have experienced or are experiencing. You are not alone. You are not an exception. Jesus knows you. He knows what it feels like to be you. He can be your faithful high priest.

> For this reason he had to be made like his brothers in every way, in order that he might become a merciful and faithful high priest in service to God, and that he might make atonement for the sins of the people. Because he himself suffered when he was tempted, he is able to help those who are being tempted. (Hebrews 2:17–18)

So, we see that not only do we participate in the fellowship of sharing in His sufferings, but He participates in the fellowship of sharing in our sufferings and temptations and weaknesses. It's a fellowship. It's a mutually felt participation with each other. He knows you, and we are coming to know Him more and more by grace through faith, by the fellowship of sharing in His sufferings and, in response, becoming like Him in His death.

– 12 –

Dying Inwardly

PHILIPPIANS 3:10–11

*It is the continual death unto self that
constitutes the life of faith.*
—François Fénelon

This brings us to the phrase, "becoming like him in his death." Paul says, and hopefully so do we: "I want to know Christ and the power of his resurrection and the fellowship of sharing in his sufferings, becoming like him in his death" (Philippians 3:10).

Becoming like Him in His death is becoming like Christ in how He reacted and responded to suffering and having to die on a cross. How Christ responded to suffering was by dying, both outwardly and inwardly. Again, we may not be called upon to die physically/outwardly for Christ—that is, to be martyred—but every one of us is called upon to die inwardly along with Christ, for Christ. And again, this dying inwardly, this letting go, is at the same time the easiest and the hardest thing to do. But we do end up doing it, over and over again. The cross always gets its way. Praise Him. It is how we attain to the resurrection from the dead = it is how we come to know greater and deeper rest = experiential oneness with Christ = bearing much fruit by just living = abiding.

Whoever serves Him must follow in His footsteps, including to Gethsemane and Golgotha. Jesus said:

> I tell you the truth, unless a kernel of wheat falls to the ground and dies, it remains only a single seed. But if it dies, it produces many seeds. The man who loves his life will lose it, while the man who hates his life in this world will keep it for eternal life. Whoever serves me must follow me; and where I am, my servant also will be. My Father will honor the one who serves me. (John 12:24–26)

Dying inwardly for Christ, dying to self, is what sanctification is all about. It is the process of being caused to let go of control, of letting go of that which "matters most," of letting go of self-will that is in opposition to God's will, at ever-deepening levels of our being. The longer we are in Christ, the longer we have walked with Him, the deeper and more subtle and more "hidden" these areas of self will be that we must let go of. This explains our unexplained suffering.

Dying to self is, at the same time, the easiest and hardest thing we are called upon to do as disciples of Christ. What we want in our spirit more than anything is that which our sinful nature fights against just as hard. This process of sanctification (Galatians 5:16–18) interprets and explains all of the mysterious inward striving and struggle we go through as Christians. We are refusing to just let go. We are refusing to give in to God in the specific area that God is dealing with in us, in those moments or days. We are probably insisting on understanding in some form instead of trusting in the Lord with *all* our heart (Proverbs 3:5–6).

Jean-Pierre de Caussade said, "Is it not, on the contrary, this resistance, which we too often continued without owning it even to ourselves which is the cause of all our troubles?"[1]

This resistance, this struggle, is a struggle against dying, against letting go of control at some deeper level that God is currently addressing. We are inwardly insisting on control, and God is working in us to let go. It is the inward experience of the cross; it is the inward experience of death by crucifixion.

The Experience of the Cross

Dead people feel no pain. There's only pain where there's still life. Where you are experiencing inward struggle, you can be sure you are going through the experience of the cross—you can be sure that God is working in you to let go of control, to die to self at some new level. This explains your inward struggle. Take heart

> *Jesus died so we could live. All He asks from us is to return the favor.*

... it is God working in you to will and to act according to His good purpose, and He always gets His way. Everything every moment is God working in you to free you from yourself (subjectively) and give you Himself. This is His "love that surpasses knowledge" (Ephesians 3:17–19). Because everything is God working in you, He is always intimately close.

A. W. Tozer said, "The cross effects its ends by destroying one established pattern, the victim's, and creating another pattern, its own. Thus it always has its way."[2] The established pattern of holding onto and insisting upon control in some form is replaced by a pattern of letting go and just living, depending upon the indwelling Holy Spirit's control. Jesus died so we could live. All He asks from us is to return the favor.

This work of the cross is something that is experienced deep within. We will not recognize what this is when it's happening or how this works without hearing and learning about it. Hopefully hearing and learning about it will help us to stop fighting against it as much as we do. We need to recognize our inward struggles as

God working in us to free us from ourselves and give us Himself (Job 7:17–19). Inward struggles (Galatians 5:16–18) are God's working in us to free us from harmful inward patterns of self-life and control and to give us His life-giving inward patterns of freedom and just living because of His control.

Consider these words of Jeanne Guyon: "We may be assured, that there is an internal [spiritual] advancement, where there is an advancement in the way of the cross. Abandonment [to Christ] and the Cross go hand in hand."[3]

Abandonment to Christ and the experience of the cross go hand in hand because it is the experience of the cross that causes abandonment to Christ. We are talking about deeply inward things here. God allows and uses suffering in our lives to bring us to deeper and deeper places of letting go of control. In other words, God allows and uses suffering in our lives to bring us to deeper and deeper places of abandonment of self to Him = dying to self. The role of suffering in sanctification is to bring us to deeper and deeper levels of brokenness, to deeper and deeper levels of letting go of, and freedom from, self-will and unbelief. This biblically and properly interprets and explains your deepest inward struggles as a Christian. (See Galatians 5:16–26; Romans 6–8.)

Where God Finds Space Created by Letting Go, He Enters

True abandonment, according to Larry Crabb, is "giving ourselves to God in utter dependence on His willingness to give Himself to us."[4]

I would change this a little. . . . Abandonment is giving myself to God in utter dependence on His ardent desire to give Himself to me. Abandonment is letting go of control, resting inwardly, and just living because I believe Jesus, who lives in me, will be filling me and living through me as I do so, because He said He would = the truth that sets us free = the New Covenant of the Spirit.

"Where God finds space He enters,"[5] says Crabb. This kind of space is created only by brokenness. Where God finds space created by brokenness, He enters. The indwelling Holy Spirit always fills in space created by brokenness with Himself. The indwelling Holy Spirit always fills in space created by dying to self with Himself. The indwelling Holy Spirit always fills in space created by letting go with Himself.

Sanctification is hard to go through because it is the process of God freeing us from—causing us to let go of—deep inward patterns and movements of self and replacing them with His own patterns and movements. Fénelon said it this way: "This is the great fast, when mortals see their poverty completely exposed, when the slightest vestige of their life in themselves is torn out by the roots."[6]

We all have inward, deeply established patterns (Tozer), movements of self-love (Fénelon), and thinking habits that must be removed and replaced. These patterns, movements of self-love, and self-interested thinking habits are the sinful nature desiring what is contrary to the Spirit. The sinful nature and the Spirit are in conflict with each other so that you do not do what you want (Galatians 5:17). But if you are led by the Spirit, you are not under law (v. 18). In those moments, yielding to the Spirit and, by the Spirit, making right choices are the solution.

Walls and Strongholds

Speaking prophetically and poetically of Jesus Christ, the psalmist says to the Lord in Psalm 89:38–41, "But you have rejected, you have spurned, you have been very angry with your anointed one. You have renounced the covenant with your servant and have defiled his crown in the dust. You have broken through all his walls and reduced his strongholds to ruins. All who pass by

have plundered him; he has become the scorn of his neighbors."
(See also 1 John 2:2.)

Jesus learned obedience from what He suffered, and so do we.
We can personalize verse 40 and understand it as describing God's
work of sanctification that He is carrying out inside of us: "You
have broken through all my walls and reduced my strongholds to
ruins."

We all have inner "walls" and "strongholds" that must be
broken through and reduced to ruins by God Himself. As
pointed out above, these are deeply established inner patterns,
movements, and thinking habits that must be destroyed and
replaced. Our loving, constantly sanctifying Father breaks
through and reduces to ruins our inward walls and strongholds in
order to replace them with Himself.

We erect interior walls to protect ourselves from exterior
threats posed by other people. We erect interior walls to protect
ourselves from interior threats posed by deeply held fears. We
have great inner strongholds, tightly held habits of thinking and
being, erected long ago to protect us once again from outer and
inner threats. In psychological circles, these walls and strongholds
would be called "defenses," and that's a good word for them. These
inward walls and strongholds are once again the sin nature's way of
trying to be in control in response to fear and feeling threatened.

The thing about walls and strongholds is that they have been
erected by us to keep threats and pain out, but they end up keeping
us in. They inevitably prevent freedom—freedom to just live and
be whole people. Breaking through our walls and reducing our
strongholds to ruins is God's work of sanctification inside of us. It
accurately interprets and explains your deepest inner battles and
resistances.

Sanctification is God Himself dealing with "sin living in me"
(Romans 7:17, 20).

Where "Intimate Purgation" Comes In

John of the Cross used these beautiful words, "intimate purgation," to describe the process of sanctification. We might say "customized sanctification." It is sanctification according to our idiosyncrasies; sanctification in those places, ways of thinking, habits, and temperament that make us different than anyone else. Sanctification in those places that only God knows about.

God's breaking of our wills, freeing us from deeply established patterns, movements of self-love, and thinking habits is where "intimate purgation" comes in. As Christians, we must understand and recognize that everything is God, that everything going on inside of us every moment, moment by moment, is God working in us to free us from ourselves and give us Himself. He never looks away from us or leaves us alone, even for an instant.

To *purge* is "to clear of moral defilement"; "to remove by cleansing." *Intimate* is "belonging to or characterizing one's deepest nature"; "marked by very close association, contact, or familiarity"; "of a very personal or private nature." So, for our purposes, we could define "intimate purgation" as "removal of moral defilement through cleansing in one's deepest nature by Someone in very close association, contact, and familiarity with us."

"Who can discern his errors? Forgive my hidden faults" (Psalm 19:12). "Hidden" faults and "sin living in me" (Romans 7:17, 20) are synonymous. Scripture is talking about deep inward patterns, movements, and thinking habits that we are not aware of and have no control over that God is freeing us from. We need to recognize inward struggles as God working in us to free us from ourselves and give us Himself.

Living with the Unknown

We know that God is "intimately acquainted" (Psalm 139:3 NASB 1995) with all our ways, all of our outer ways and all of our inner ways. He knows all of our harmful inward patterns, movements, and thinking habits. Our Father created our inmost being and knit us together in our mother's womb (v. 13). When He wove us together in our mother's womb, His eyes saw our unformed body (vv. 15–16). He knows us because He created us, inside and out. He knows us because He created our inmost being. Knitting each of us together in our mother's womb implies focus, attention to detail, time, affectionate care—with no two human beings exactly alike and no mistakes made on God's part. No wonder our sanctification is intimately private and personal, and hardly understood, even by ourselves (Isaiah 55:8–9).

When we don't understand what's going on, we still trust, we trust God Himself for who He is. He knows. He knows what He's doing. He knows everything already. He *knows* you. What else could possibly be needed?

Although he has no idea why he is suffering the way he is, Job unwittingly describes intimate purgation in his prayer to God in 7:17–19. "What is man that you make so much of him, that you give him so much attention, that you examine him every morning and test him every moment? Will you never look away from me, or let me alone even for an instant?" Most likely none of us will go through the intensity and severity of Job's trials, but intimate purgation can still be very tough to go through. Perhaps the most painful part is our lack of understanding, our lack of knowledge of what's going on, our lack of ability to do something to change things. At first, we desperately, frantically try to change things, to discover what it is we're doing wrong, or not doing right, so we can fix it and get relief. This is not the proper response to our suffering. This is not "becoming like him in his death" (Philippians 3:10).

Often the hardest part of intimate purgation is living with the unknown. God uses unexplained trials and suffering to purge us deeply and intimately of habits of self that we are not even aware of. All we can do is trust, wait, and humble ourselves under His mighty hand that He may lift us up in due time. And the God of all grace, who called us to His eternal glory in Christ, after we have suffered a little while, will Himself restore us and make us strong, firm, and steadfast (1 Peter 5:6, 10). He did this with Job, and He will do it with us.

Not a Perpetual Struggle of the Head

If we were simply letting go and yielding (Romans 6:11–14) all of the time, we would be filled and controlled all of the time by the indwelling Holy Spirit, and we would be loving, joyful, peaceful, patient, kind, good, faithful, gentle, and self-controlled all of the time. Thus the answer to all of our inward struggles and wrestling is letting go/yielding to the indwelling ready-to-fill-and-control Holy Spirit. This is what dying to self is. Dying to self is an inward letting go.

"Jesus called out with a loud voice, 'Father, into your hands I commit my spirit.' When he had said this, he breathed his last" (Luke 23:46). Dying to self means letting go of control at ever-deepening levels of our being in the midst of not understanding and not being able to change what's going on.

Jesus learned obedience from what He suffered, and so do we.

Fénelon wrote, "While you labor less you will do many more useful things. It is not a question of a perpetual struggle of the head."[7] Let me explain that "while you labor" means striving in your head to understand so that you can feel in control. The psalmist put it this way: "When I tried to understand all this, it was oppressive to me" (Psalm 73:16). The point is to cease striving, not to perpetually struggle in your mind to understand.

Letting go of this "perpetual struggle of the head" is mainly what is meant by dying to self = just living. You'll know this perpetual struggle of the head when you're doing it. Some of you have been enslaved to it for years. I was. Compulsive thinking and insisting on understanding is a common form of sin living in me, that is, in my sinful nature. Compulsive anything is hard to let go of. But with God all things are possible (Matthew 19:26).

In His perfect way, in His perfect timing, God Himself brings you to the place of letting go, through suffering. "I want to know Christ . . . and the fellowship of sharing in his sufferings, becoming like him in his death" (Philippians 3:10). Jesus learned obedience from what He suffered, and so do we. Jesus learned submission of His will to the will of Another from what He suffered, and so do we (Hebrews 5:7–10; Mark 14:35–36).

Galatians 5:18 and Romans 6:14

At this time, please read carefully and compare Galatians 5:18 and Romans 6:14. They are saying the same thing and offering the same solution to the problem of sin. The reason sin shall not be our master is because we are under the grace of being controlled and led by the indwelling, filling Holy Spirit now. So just yield; so just live. He will be filling (Ephesians 5:18), controlling (Romans 8:9), and living through us (John 15:5) as we just live. This is what it means to be led by the Spirit so that we're no longer under law. The control of the Holy Spirit in us is the grace we are under that prevents sin from being our master. So simply yield to what is and just live.

Regarding this Galatians 5:16–18 inward battle for control, you will often find yourself stymied or somewhat "paralyzed" in the midst of this inner battle. You cannot/do not do what you want (v. 17). The desires of the sinful nature fundamentally have to do with wanting control, or at least a subjective feeling of being the one in control. The sinful nature desires control, and the Spirit in us desires control. The inner battle is one of fighting for a feeling of control due to fear and unbelief versus simply and confidently letting go in those moments to the indwelling Holy Spirit, who also wants control.

The good news is that (1) this battle is happening because God is bringing you to a new level of faith and freedom, and (2) God always wins in His perfect timing—the cross always gets its way (Tozer). You will yield; you will become like Him in His death (Luke 23:44–46). You will cease striving and thereby know that He is God, not you (Psalm 46:10).

This inward battle of Galatians 5:16–18 is the experience of the cross that Christians go through to some extent every day. It is how sanctification works. Sanctification is the fellowship of sharing in His sufferings and, in response to these sufferings, becoming like Him in His death. In this way, somehow, we attain to the resurrection from the dead in order to know experiential oneness with Christ now, in this life. That is what sanctification is. The Galatians 5:16–18 battle is an everyday event . . . losing it doesn't have to be. (See Romans 7:14–8:4.)

We Are Making Progress, by Grace Through Faith

Dying on the cross is something we experience inwardly as Christians. It is "becoming like Him in His death." But, as I said, what we want in our spirit more than anything—that is, to die to self so that Christ can completely fill us—our sin nature fights against just as hard. But the good news is that the cross always gets its way = in this process of sanctification, God Himself always gets His way.

We are His beloved children. His love and faithfulness are such that, in this process of sanctification, in the wisdom of God's loving discipline of His legitimate children, He always wins, and we *are* making progress. "If God is for us, who can be against us?" (Romans 8:31). We can read this verse this way: If

God, the Maker and Ruler of heaven and earth and us, is *for* us—is on our side in this battle—who can possibly be against us? Who can possibly thwart what He has chosen to do for us, in us and through us? Who can possibly thwart His plans for us? Not even we can do this to ourselves. And His plans and purpose are that we be conformed to the likeness of His Son (Romans 8:28–29).

As the apostle Paul wrote to the Corinthians: "Now the Lord is the Spirit, and where the Spirit of the Lord is, there is freedom. And we, who with unveiled faces all reflect the Lord's glory, are being transformed into his likeness with ever-increasing glory, which comes from the Lord, who is the Spirit" (2 Corinthians 3:17–18).

When our church meets, we often sing a hymn that proclaims God is making all things new, even in places we don't choose.[8] Exactly. In places we don't choose, He makes all things new, and it's hard to go through. We don't choose these places partly because we don't even know they're there. They are "sin living in me" (Romans 7:17, 20). Even if we did know about them, we, in and of ourselves, would not choose to go through what it takes to free us from them, even though we might know it is for our own good. In our own selves, in our own self-loving self, in our sinful nature, we are quite content to stay right where we are in our spiritual advancement as long as we're reasonably comfortable there. We don't like change. But God has something better for us that we don't know about. God Himself living in us, by grace through faith, causes and enables us to choose and endure the deep, inward, painful experience of change that He is working in us (Galatians 5:17; Hebrews 5:7–10) because He has predestined us to be conformed to the likeness of His Son. As the psalmist said about suffering: "My comfort in my suffering is this: Your promise preserves my life" (Psalm 119:50).

It is because of God's love that surpasses knowledge (Ephesians 3:19) that He chooses to free us from ourselves and give us Himself in places we don't choose, and never would choose. This freedom is what results in fullness of joy, and God has willed to give it to us, even when we, in our ignorance, fight Him on it because we are satisfied to stay where we are. Our self-love puts our own "good enough" far ahead of any willingness to go through what it takes to be freed from ourselves and more conformed to the likeness of Christ. Thank God for His love that surpasses knowledge, that He never looks away from us nor leaves us alone even for an instant.

God Never Fails

God accomplishes in us, for us, and through us that which He has planned for us, not because we get it right and cooperate but because He has chosen to and chooses to. His love is unfailing in accomplishing in us, for us, and through us what He has planned and predestined for us. Like Abraham, we are "children of promise." The Lord promised to the children of Israel, "I *will* remove from you your heart of stone and give you a heart of flesh. And I *will* put my Spirit in you and [cause] you to follow my decrees and be careful to keep my laws" (Ezekiel 36:26–27, emphasis mine).

Thankfully, He always wins because He has willed it so for us (Romans 8:31–32). The cross always gets its way because we are predestined to be conformed to the likeness of Jesus. That is what is going on in all your struggles. You need look no further than God's love that surpasses knowledge: "And we know that in all things God works for the good of those who love him, who have been called according to his purpose. For those God foreknew he also predestined to be conformed to the likeness of his Son, that he might be the firstborn among many brothers" (Romans 8:28–29).

You've been predestined to be conformed to the likeness of His Son by God Himself, so just live. Just live and stop thinking about yourself and how you're behaving so much. Count yourself dead to sin and alive to God in Christ Jesus and just live.

We know that in *all* things God works for the good of those who love Him. All things means all things. God Himself must do it and He does. He does succeed in breaking our stubborn, control-wanting self-wills. He does succeed in freeing us from "sin living in me" at ever-deepening levels of our being, because of love, because He is faithful, because He chooses to, because He has predestined us to be conformed to the likeness of His Son more and more in this life.

The Experience of the Cross, Outwardly and Inwardly

When someone was dying on a Roman cross back in Christ's day, what they wanted in their spirit more than anything was death and the freedom death would bring from the awful suffering they were experiencing. Yet, at the same time, they would struggle to live by using their legs to raise themselves up so they could take a life-giving breath, over and over again, up and down . . . up and down. The way they would finally die is that a soldier would come by and break the victim's legs. This way he couldn't push up anymore and he suffocated. What the victim wanted more than anything . . . freedom from suffering that came by death . . . something else inside of him fought against just as hard. This is Romans 7:14–25 and Galatians 5:16–18. It is the experience of the cross.

All disciples of Christ will go through this battle as they just live. However, again, the battle is inevitable . . . losing it is not (Galatians 5:18). By grace through faith, we become better and better at living by the Spirit. By grace through faith, we become better and better at becoming like Him in His death, and so, somehow, attaining to the resurrection from the dead, in *this* life.

The Solution Is Letting Go and Just Living

Larry Crabb explains it this way: "The search to discover God requires that we *abandon* ourselves, that we give up control of what matters most, and that we place our *confidence* in Someone we cannot manage. These requirements are as vital as they are difficult."[9]

> The crucial need in the church is an understanding of living by the Spirit.

This is the battle going on within us. This is the inward battle of Galatians 5:16–18. This is the inward battle going on in Romans 7:14–25. It is the battle between the indwelling Holy Spirit and the sin nature. The victory comes from letting go, from dying = yielding to the Spirit = letting go of control to the control of the indwelling Holy Spirit.

And, because the Holy Spirit is now the dominant force within you, the yielding is simply a yielding to what is; the letting go is simply a letting go. It is simply a dying. (See the diagram on p. 49.) All letting go is letting go to God because He is the one living in you and controlling you now. So just live.

The crucial need in the church is an understanding of living by the Spirit. Galatians 5:16 says, "So I say, live by the Spirit, and you will not gratify the desires of the sinful nature." Living by the Spirit = just living because He is the one controlling you now, because you no longer live but He lives in you, because you are simply and only a branch in the Vine, because you are one with Him now, because He *is* your life now.

As you are living by the Spirit through faith, you will not be gratifying the desires of the sinful nature. As you are believing Romans 8:9, as you are simply counting upon this fact and therefore just living, you will not be gratifying the desires of the sinful nature. "Then you will know the truth, and the truth will set you free" (John 8:32; see also John 8:31–36). Living by the Spirit is the truth Jesus is talking about. (See Galatians 5:16.) Then you will know the truth, that you are controlled by the Spirit now, and this truth will set you free, free from sin as a way of life, free from the law and free "indeed," free to just live and be yourself and see righteousness and fruit as the norm as you're doing so.

It is good to know what the Holy Spirit is doing inside of us and how suffering fits in. Suffering causes us to let go and just live, to let go of control at ever-deepening levels of our being so we can be filled up and controlled by Him more and more fully = the fellowship of sharing in His sufferings, becoming like Him in His death. Jesus learned obedience from what He suffered, and so do we. Obedience is reverent submission of my will to the will of Another, and we must be caused to do it.

Jesus was the perfect Spirit-filled man. He, of course, needed no sanctification. His will and the Father's will were always perfectly one, as most pointedly expressed in Mark 14:36. We are not perfectly Spirit-filled men and women yet. We have not attained perfect experiential oneness with Christ yet. We have not yet attained to the resurrection from the dead (Philippians 3:12–14), but it is where God is bringing us. For us, becoming like Him in His death is dying to self, letting go of control at whatever level God is dealing with us. It is "reverent submission" (Hebrews 5:7). We are learning reverent submission to God's will by what we suffer.

Those "Thousand Reflections by Which We Wrap and Bury Ourselves in Self"

Fénelon wrote, "Do not reason too much, always have an upright purpose in the smallest matters, and pay no attention to the thousand reflections by which we wrap and bury ourselves in self, under pretense of correcting our faults."[10]

Often our desire for control during these inward battles with fear, doubt, and temptation to give up the faith takes on the form of compulsive thinking. Asaph is guilty of this in Psalm 73.

In the midst of his insistence on understanding, in the midst of his dependence on his own thinking and reasoning, Asaph cries out, "When I tried to understand all this, it was oppressive to me" (Psalm 73:16). Likewise, insistence upon understanding and dependence on our own human reasoning will only lead to greater inner turmoil and frustration.

This thinking, this insisting on understanding, this trying to understand in our heads, which becomes more and more oppressive, is a natural sin-nature response to fear. It reveals whatever it is we are putting our trust in other than God, which is self. We inwardly insist on figuring things out. What is really going on is an insistence on understanding in order to feel better. Again, this is simply an effort to gain a sense of control. It only makes things worse. We must die to this. Asaph didn't gain peace "till I entered the sanctuary of God" (v. 17). It is only in humbling oneself and letting go of insistence on control, in the form of insistence on understanding, that we find peace. We must let go and just live = enter the sanctuary of God = surrender to the Spirit = let go of insistence on figuring it out = surrender to the control of the Spirit. This all also comes from God, as He shows us truth and gives us faith in it.

You will recognize the difference between your own compulsive insistence-type thinking and "the mind controlled by the Spirit" thinking. Godly thinking is characterized by "life and peace" (Romans 8:6). Your own compulsive, insistent, dependent-on-self type of thinking will be accompanied by greater frustration, "oppression" (Psalm 73:16), getting nowhere, sleeplessness, increased heart rate, increased body temperature, and maybe even cold sweats. The more you attempt to cling to it, the worse it will get. Read Psalm 131. Like a weaned child with its mother, we must learn to let go and just live. A lot of Christians today are overthinking rather than resting in God. A lot of serious Christians today are enslaved to this overthinking, and their confidence is in it. I used to be one of them. There is a difference between living by the Spirit and living by the head. "But the mind controlled by the Spirit is life and peace" (Romans 8:6).

Counting on God's Active Presence Within Us

The active presence of God working inside of us, freeing us from ourselves and giving us Himself, explains everything. He never looks away from us or leaves us alone, even for an instant. His love surpasses knowledge. "What is man that you make so much of him, that you give him so much attention, that you examine him every morning and test him every moment?" (Job 7:17–18). The testing is to see if I'll die at this new hidden level at which He is working to free me from myself and give me Himself. To pass the test, I yield to His Spirit by just living (Galatians 5:18). I let go of fighting Him and just live, knowing that He will fill me up, live through me, and control me as I do so.

– 13 –

And So Do We

HEBREWS 5:7–10

The will of God has nothing but sweetness, favours and
treasures for submissive souls; it is impossible to repose too
much confidence in it, nor to abandon oneself to it too utterly.
—Jean-Pierre de Caussade

We have in Hebrews a key passage to understanding what Paul means by "becoming like Him in His death" in Philippians 3:10:

> During the days of Jesus' life on earth, he offered up prayers and petitions with loud cries and tears to the one who could save him from death, and he was heard because of his reverent submission. Although he was a son, he learned obedience from what he suffered and, once made perfect, he became the source of eternal salvation for all who obey him and was designated by God to be high priest in the order of Melchizedek. (Hebrews 5:7–10)

Of course, verse 7 of this passage reminds us of Jesus's agony in the Garden of Gethsemane just before His arrest and crucifixion.

> Jesus went out as usual to the Mount of Olives, and his disciples followed him. On reaching the place, he said

to them, "Pray that you will not fall into temptation." He withdrew about a stone's throw beyond them, knelt down and prayed, "Father, if you are willing, take this cup from me; yet not my will, but yours be done." An angel from heaven appeared to him and strengthened him. And being in anguish, he prayed more earnestly, and his sweat was like drops of blood falling to the ground. (Luke 22:39–44)

But this kind of praying by Jesus did not happen only once. Hebrews 5:7 begins, "During the days of Jesus' life on earth." Notice that the word *days* is plural. The implication is that there were many times that Jesus prayed this way, "with loud cries and tears," to the One who could save Him from death. Jesus knew the death He was going to die. For at least the three years of His earthly ministry, Jesus lived every day with the knowledge of how He was going to die. He lived every day with the knowledge of how, for the first time since eternity past, He was going to experience separation from, rejection by, and broken fellowship with the Father. This knowledge of how and why He was going to die loomed before Him for most, if not all, of His earthly life.

I believe this was what was most agonizing for Him—the coming reality that, for the first and only time since eternity past, fellowship and glorious experiential oneness with the Father was going to be broken. This coming reality that fellowship with the Father was going to be broken, even for only a few hours, was what caused Jesus the greatest anguish. This was what made His upcoming death nearly intolerable.

Opportune Times for Temptation and Prayer in Lonely Places

We read in Luke 4 about Jesus's temptation in the desert by the devil after eating nothing for forty days. Verse 13 says,

"When the devil had finished all this tempting, he left him *until an opportune time*" (emphasis mine). We can be sure that the devil recognized and took advantage of many "opportune times" during Jesus's three-year ministry with His disciples. Just as with us, these would have been times when Jesus, in His humanness, was exhausted, threatened by evil men, rejected by enemies and former followers, criticized and accused and misunderstood and thronged by self-seeking, needy people.

Luke also tells us that Jesus "often" left the disciples and the crowds of people clamoring for His attention to go off by Himself to a lonely place to pray. "Yet the news about him spread all the more, so that crowds of people came to hear him and to be healed of their sicknesses. But Jesus often withdrew to lonely places and prayed" (Luke 5:15–16).

So we have Satan looking for opportune times to harass and tempt Jesus, and we have Jesus often withdrawing from the people to go to lonely places to pray. It is likely that many of these were times of prayers and petitions offered up with loud cries and tears to the One who could save Him from death. To the degree that we understand the Psalms as much of Jesus's prayer language, we see Him pouring out His heart regarding betrayal, injustice, loneliness, and pleas for deliverance. Isaiah tells us, "He was despised and rejected by men, a man of sorrows, and familiar with suffering" (Isaiah 53:3). To be despised and rejected by men was common and painful. To be despised and rejected by His Father was once and cataclysmic.

Jesus Was Heard by His Father

"And He was heard because of His reverent submission" (Hebrews 5:7). What does this mean that Jesus was heard because of His reverent submission? Obviously Jesus still died and was buried in a tomb. Jesus still cried out, "My God, my God, why have you forsaken me?" After this, "he cried out in a loud voice" and "breathed his last." (See Mark 15:34–37.) Jesus did die and was buried in a tomb. But, as the NIV text note regarding Hebrews 5:7 says, "His prayer was granted by the Father, who saved him from death—through resurrection."[1] God did not abandon Him to the grave nor allow His Holy One to see decay (Psalm 16:10).

God answered Jesus's prayer; Jesus was heard. During some of those prayer times in some lonely place, I'm sure Jesus rejoiced this way. He rejoiced in remembering, reciting, and praying the verses below, knowing that, just like the passages and verses about His death, these verses and this truth were also certain: "Therefore my heart is glad and my tongue rejoices; my body also will rest secure, because you will not abandon me to the grave, nor will you let your Holy One see decay. You have made known to me the path of life; you will fill me with joy in your presence, with eternal pleasures at your right hand" (Psalm 16:9–11).

And maybe Jesus thought in His mind or even added out loud, "Once again, just as You always have . . . just like it has always been, it will be again. Oh Abba, Father, thank you, thank you, thank you."

So, Jesus was heard. He was heard "because of his reverent submission." What reverent submission and when? Once again, in our mind we are brought to Jesus's praying in the Garden of Gethsemane just before His arrest and eventual crucifixion.

> They went to a place called Gethsemane, and Jesus said to his disciples, "Sit here while I pray." He took Peter, James and John along with him, and he began to be deeply distressed and troubled. "My soul is overwhelmed with sorrow to the point of death," he said to them. "Stay here and keep watch." Going a little farther, he fell to the ground and prayed that if possible the hour might pass from him. "Abba, Father," he said, "everything is possible for you. Take this cup from me. Yet not what I will, but what you will." (Mark 14:32–36)

We have in this last sentence the greatest expression of reverent submission ever uttered.

The Ultimate Conundrum

Part of what makes Jesus's prayer the greatest expression of reverent submission ever uttered is that we also have in these few verses the ultimate conundrum, the ultimate seeming contradiction, the ultimate temptation to doubt the Father's love. Therefore, Jesus's response to this temptation, "Yet not what I will, but what you will," is the greatest occasion of reverent submission and trust ever expressed and lived.

Jesus knew that everything is possible with God. God never *has* to do anything. He never *has* to do anything a certain way. God is not constrained by any circumstances or anything outside of Himself... there isn't anything outside of Himself or outside of His complete control and will. He *could* have done it differently.

Everything is possible for Him. In no way, shape, or form did God *have* to do it the way He was doing it, and Jesus knew this. In saying, "Everything is possible for you," Jesus is saying, "You *could* do this differently ... yet not what I will but what you will." This is the ultimate perfect trust (Proverbs 3:5–6).

> Everything *is possible with God.*

In His human state, there indeed was some mystery here for Jesus, some lack of knowledge, some lack of understanding, another instance of only God the Father knowing. (See Matthew 24:36; Mark 13:32.) Perhaps this was one of those "opportune times" (Luke 4:13) that the devil sorely tempted Jesus, the temptation to doubt the Father's love.

When we go through times of severe trial and excruciating outward or inward pain, it just doesn't seem to make sense. After all, God *could* intervene. He could have prevented it ... everything is possible for Him ... but He didn't. We are tempted to doubt God's love. Yet, we also know that "we do not have a high priest who is unable to sympathize with our weaknesses, but we have one who has been tempted in every way, just as we are—yet was without sin" (Hebrews 4:15). So we "fix our eyes on Jesus, the author and perfecter of our faith, who for the joy set before him endured the cross, scorning its shame, and sat down at the right hand of the throne of God" (Hebrews 12:2).

If there was ever a time for Jesus to be tempted to doubt the Father's love, this was it. Jesus didn't *have* to go to the cross. *Everything* is possible with God. God *could* have done it differently. But He chose not to. He chose for His Son to go to the cross. He chose to do it this way. He chose to let His Son suffer, and He chooses to let us suffer sometimes, outwardly and inwardly, just like Jesus. This outward and inward suffering is part of what it means to be a disciple of Christ. Like Jesus, it's how we "learn obedience" (Hebrews 5:8). Jesus learned obedience from what He suffered, and so do we. "It is the fire of suffering," said Jeanne Guyon, "that brings forth the gold of godliness."[2]

Jesus trusted His Father in the midst of His suffering, and He worshipped. The essence of worship is surrender. "Yet not what I will, but what you will" (Mark 14:36). Jesus reverently submitted to and trusted in His Father's will. In His humanness, by the Spirit, Jesus trusted in the Lord with all His heart and leaned not on His own understanding (Proverbs 3:5).

When We're Tempted to Doubt

By God's grace, we too can live this way. At those times when things don't make sense and seem contradictory, we cannot confine God to the limits of our finite, created minds. He knows more than we do. He knows what He's doing when we don't. Consider what God tells us in Isaiah 55:8–9: " 'For my thoughts are not your thoughts, neither are your ways my ways,' declares the LORD. 'As the heavens are higher than the earth, so are my ways higher than your ways, and my thoughts than your thoughts.' "

That's *much* higher. How foolish to doubt Him and His love because, to our mind, there's some apparent contradiction, or maybe the way He is doing things isn't the way we would do them. How foolish to doubt Him and His love when His way doesn't seem logical or rational or just or fair or loving or understandable. The fact is that His ways are much, much "higher" than our ways and His thoughts much, much "higher" than our thoughts. So we must reverently submit to His will in everything. It is foolish not to do so. Jesus was heard "because of his reverent submission," and so are we. We have been, are, and will be resurrected.

We must remember that this reverent submission, like Jesus's offering up prayers and petitions with loud cries and tears, was not a one-time event at Gethsemane. Just as the devil tempted Jesus throughout His life and ministry at "opportune times," and just as Jesus "often withdrew to lonely places and prayed," so His reverent submission was a lifestyle and daily choice. Jesus lived moment by moment submitted to the will of His Father. He and His Father were one. Jesus lived in oneness of will with His Father (John 17:20–23; 14:9–11, 20–21). He lived His life submitted to His oneness with the Father, and so can we. Our oneness with the Father and the Son is our whole and only source of being able to say, "Yet not what I will, but what You will."

Knowing, living in, counting upon, and surrendering to our oneness with the Father and the Son is also our key to surviving times of severe temptation to doubt. Letting go of our finite human reasoning because of the fact of Isaiah 55:8–9, letting go to our oneness with the Father and the Son, letting go to God Himself because He knows more than we do, letting go and just living in that moment of severe temptation to doubt God's presence and love is how we survive it. "Yet not what I will, but what you will" (Mark 14:36). The more you insist on understanding at these times, the more oppressive it will become (Psalm 73:16). Your feet will almost slip; you will nearly lose your foothold (Psalm 73:2).

Our Oneness with Christ and the Father Is Our Whole and Only Source of Strength

We must come to realize and count upon the fact that we too have been brought into and are now included in this oneness with Jesus and the Father that He talks about in John: "Don't you believe that I am in the Father, and that the Father is in me? The words I say to you are not just my own. Rather, it is the Father, living in me, who is doing his work" (John 14:10).

Likewise, we are in Jesus and the Father, and Jesus and the Father are in us. The words we speak and the works we do are not our own. Rather, it is Jesus and the Father living in us who are doing their work in and through us as we abide, as we just live.

> My prayer is not for them alone. I pray also for those who will believe in me through their message, that all of them may be one, Father, just as you are in me and I am in you. May they also be in us so that the world may believe that you have sent me. I have given them the glory that you gave me that they may be one as we are one: I in them and you in me.
> (John 17:20–23)

Oneness with each other comes only when individual Christians fully know and abide in their oneness with the Father and the Son.

F. J. Huegel said, "This principle of participation—oneness with Christ—has reaches so unfathomable that not even the spiritual man finds it easy to scale the heights and grasp its full meaning. We stand overawed. We stagger. Faith wavers."[3]

Jesus lived in continual reverent submission to the Father and His will in everything so that when He experienced the greatest test of His faith and greatest temptation to distrust and doubt the Father and His love, Jesus was able to pass the test by submitting to the will of His Father, by letting go to His oneness with the Father (Mark 14:35–36).

Jesus's oneness with the Father was His whole source of strength to get through His suffering. Likewise, our oneness with the Father and the Son is our whole and only source of strength to get through our suffering. "I can do everything through him who gives me strength" (Philippians 4:13). What Paul means is "I can do everything through my oneness with Christ; I can do and endure all things through Christ living in me, giving me His strength." Jesus does not send strength down from heaven, from far away outside of us somewhere. He lives inside of us in the person of the Holy Spirit and, living there, He *is* our strength (Psalm 73:26).

Paul also means things this way in 2 Corinthians 12:9–10. Jesus's grace is sufficient for us from His place living inside of us. When we are weak in ourselves, He is strongest inside of us. This is the grace He is talking about. When we are weak, we are strong because of His living inside of us. Jesus living inside of us *is* our strength. Yes, my flesh and my heart will fail, but God is the strength of my heart and my portion forever, because that's where He lives . . . in my heart.

When I'm depending on my flesh and my heart, I will fail. When I'm depending on my oneness with Christ, I can do all things through Him who gives me strength. His power is made perfect in my weakness. When I am weak in myself, I am strong, because of the grace of His living in and through me as I just live.

Philippians 4:13; Psalm 73:26; and 2 Corinthians 12:9–10 are all saying the same thing. They are teaching the same truth of Christ living inside of us, of oneness with Christ being our whole and only source of strength, strength to be able to reverently submit and strength to be able to do and endure all things.

Our Father's Will for Us Is Always Good, Even When It Hurts

Jesus lived reverently submitted, which enabled Him to die reverently submitted. As we live reverently submitted, we will be able to die daily, reverently submitted, and will be able to die finally, reverently submitted. Let me share with you a stanza from a beautiful old hymn, "Day by Day and with Each Passing Moment."

> Day by day, and with each passing moment,
> Strength I find, to meet my trials here;
> Trusting in my Father's wise bestowment,
> I've no cause for worry or for fear.
> He whose heart is kind beyond all measure,
> Gives unto each day what He deems best—
> Lovingly, its part of pain and pleasure,
> Mingling toil with peace and rest.[4]

Reverent submission to the Father is reverent submission to His will for us, no matter what it is. And whatever happens each day, whatever happens each moment of each day, is His will for us. It is loving and it is what is best for us, especially when it doesn't seem so. Reverent submission is recognizing, as did Jean-Pierre de Caussade, that even in trials we cannot understand, "the will of God has nothing but sweetness, favours and treasures for submissive souls."[5]

Jesus knew this. (See Mark 14:35–36.) As we just live, and thereby are being filled and controlled by the indwelling Holy Spirit, so can we.

God's Will Is That We Be Controlled by His Spirit

Reverent submission is continual, moment-by-moment surrender to the control of the indwelling, filling Holy Spirit. Reverent submission is just living so He can be filling. This is God's will for us.

> Be very careful, then, how you live—not as unwise but as wise, making the most of every opportunity, because the days are evil. Therefore do not be foolish, but understand what the Lord's will is. [Here it is . . .] Do not get drunk on wine, which leads to debauchery. Instead, be filled with the Spirit. Speak to one another with psalms, hymns and spiritual songs. Sing and make music in your heart to the Lord, always giving thanks to God the Father for everything, in the name of our Lord Jesus Christ. (Ephesians 5:15–20)

The verb tense in verses 18–20 is present tense ongoing, so it should be read, "Instead, be being filled with the Spirit, speaking to one another with psalms, hymns and spiritual songs, singing and making melody in your heart to the Lord, always giving thanks to God the Father for everything, in the name of our Lord Jesus Christ."

This wording better expresses the truth that joy, even in suffering, and thankfulness for "everything," including times of trouble and hardship, can only be our response and experience as we are being filled and controlled by the indwelling, reigning Holy Spirit.

"Always giving thanks to God the Father for everything" is simply another way of acknowledging and submitting to the fact that everything that is coming into your life is God's loving will. This is what Jesus did, even in the face of His upcoming humiliation and torturous death. We can only live this way as we are being filled, as we are being controlled by the Holy Spirit, as we are submitted to and counting upon the fact of the Holy Spirit's control in our lives and therefore just living. It is only by this reverent submission to the control of the Holy Spirit that we're able to reverently submit to the will of the Father moment by moment, day by day, no matter what that will is. It is only by the Spirit that we'll be increasingly able to submit to the will of the Father, no matter what He is allowing into our lives that moment and that day and, in addition, beginning to be able to sincerely thank Him for whatever it is He's willing and allowing.

This is supernatural living; only Jesus can live it. The New Covenant of the Spirit is His living His life in you, for you, and through you, for His own sake and the sake of others as you just live. You no longer live, but He lives in you. Living by the Spirit means counting upon this fact and resting in it. With the gospel of the New Covenant of the Spirit, if it seems too good to be true, it is true.

Jesus Learned Obedience from What He Suffered

"Although he was a son, he learned obedience from what he suffered and, once made perfect, he became the source of eternal salvation for all who obey him and was designated by God to be high priest in the order of Melchizedek" (Hebrews 5:8–10).

Although Jesus was a son, although He was one with the Father, He learned obedience from what He suffered. He learned reverent submission from what He suffered, and so do we. Reverent submission *is* obedience. At its core, in its essence, obedience is submission of my will to the will of another, to the will of Another. "Yet not what I will, but what You will" (Mark

14:36) is our way of life and death, death to self and final physical death.

Reverent submission and obedience are synonymous. Obedience is first and foremost an inward attitude, choice, decision, and behavior of yielding, yielding to the One who lives in us and yearns to live through us as we just live. This submission then results in outward acts of obedience to God and His Word because when and as we yield, He moves us, causes us (Ezekiel 36:26–27), fills us (Ephesians 5:18), controls us (Romans 8:9), and lives through us (John 15:5) because He chooses to . . . because He is

Scripture accurately explains and interprets all our experiences, both outward and inward, and instructs us in how to respond to them.

the Vine and we are the branches. God does what He says He will do. He moves in us as we just live, and we obey that moving = living by the Spirit.

"And so he condemned sin in sinful man, in order that the righteous requirements of the law might be fully met in us, who do not live according to the sinful nature but according to the Spirit" (Romans 8:3–4). This would be a good time to once again refer to, dwell on, and rejoice in the Romans 6 diagram (p. 49).

Jesus learned obedience from what He suffered. Not that He was ever disobedient. It's just that He had never existed in human form before, with a human nature. He had never existed "separate" from the Father before, in human flesh. This was all new. Because of this separation, because of this strange and different "apartness," because of this strange and different sense and existence as an "individual," with His own will apart from the Father and a capacity to exercise it (Mark 14:36), Jesus had to "learn" obedience. Jesus had to learn this submission of His will to the will of Another. Jesus learned it and did it perfectly.

James Strong defines "learn" as "to experience firsthand and by experience make it one's own." It is much more and much deeper than mere memorization of facts. Learning truth, learning those things that really matter in life, is inward and involves our whole being. We learn truth and right values (or wrong ones) and character from experiencing other people and, as Christians, from experiencing God. As Larry Crabb put it, "Change depends on experiencing the character of God."[6]

Christians Learn Obedience from What They Suffer

We learn obedience from experiencing suffering. Jesus learned obedience from what He suffered, and so do we. As disciples of Christ, learning obedience, learning reverent submission, interprets and explains every moment of suffering we go through outwardly and inwardly (Romans 8:28–29; Job 7:17–19). Scripture accurately explains and interprets all our experiences, both outward and inward, and instructs us in how to respond to them.

Jesus learned obedience from what He suffered because, in His human form, He was confronted with situations, trials, and temptations He had never experienced before. For the first and only time since eternity past, He experienced the potential and temptation to exercise His will in opposition to the Father's in ways that He never experienced before. And the temptations were very grievous.

Jesus had to learn deeper and greater submission to the Father's will in ways and at levels He had never had to learn it before, and it was the Father's will that He learn it through suffering so that He could be a faithful and sympathetic high priest in the order of Melchizedek (Hebrews 5:8–10).

Jesus learned obedience from what He suffered, and so do we. He learned "reverent submission" to the will of the Father from what He suffered, and so do we. He learned dying to self and letting go of self-will from what He suffered, and so do we. We have to learn it this way because we were born with a sinful nature that is alive and well within us.

Like Jesus, we learn submission, we learn letting go, we learn letting go of self-will, we learn dying, we learn dying to self, and we learn absolute surrender from what we suffer. We learn deeper and deeper surrender to the will of the Father from what we suffer.

To quote Larry Crabb again, "Brokenness allows us to relax in the arms that will bring us to shore,"—every time, no matter what.[7]

Sanctification and Suffering

Sanctification is the process of being lovingly, patiently forced to let go of control at deeper and deeper levels of our being. It is an inward purging and it hurts. It is a letting go, a letting go that God causes, a letting go that only God can bring about in us. And He does bring it about because He chooses to, because we have been predestined to be conformed to the likeness of His Son. Because God's love is unfailing in doing in us, for us, and through us that which He has predetermined to do, we may go through many times of failure and near-failure first, but we are eventually delivered from ourselves experientially. (See Romans 7:14–25.)

"As it is, it is no longer I myself who do it, but it is sin living in me" (Romans 7:17). We are helpless to change this inward reality.

"Now if I do what I do not want to do, it is no longer I who do it, but it is sin living in me that does it" (Romans 7:20). Refer to the diagram on page 49 as you read these verses.

"For in my inner being I delight in God's law; but I see another law [controlling power] at work in the members of my body, waging war against the law [controlling power] of my mind [which is now the Holy Spirit in me] and making me a prisoner [experientially] of the law [controlling power] of sin at work within my members" (Romans 7:22–23).

Again, the answer is Romans 8:2: "Because through Christ Jesus the law [controlling power] of the Spirit of life set me free from the law [controlling power] of sin and death."

The key to experiencing this freedom from sin is living by the Spirit through faith (Galatians 5:16–18) = just living, because we already are controlled by the Spirit (Romans 8:9 and see diagram) = "free indeed." (See John 8:31–36.)

Jesus learned (recall James Strong's definition) obedience from what He suffered, and so do we.

Listen to the prayer of Jeanne Guyon: "Hadst Thou, O my God, spared the strokes of Thy hammer, I should never have been formed to Thy will, to be an instrument for Thy use; for I was ridiculously vain."[8]

One can and should realize and pray this personally. What word or words would you place at the end of this confession? Perhaps it would be "vain" or maybe something else. For me I would have to pray, "Had You, O my God, spared the strokes of Your hammer, I would never have been formed to Your will, to be an instrument for Your use; for I was ridiculously fearful and compulsive."

Sanctification and God's Discipline

We are reminded of Hebrews 12:7: "Endure hardship as discipline; God is treating you as sons [and daughters]. For what son is not disciplined by his father?"

We have to be made to give in. The good news is that we pose no problem for God, no matter how strong our will. This is the role of suffering and the place of discipline, to cause us to let go of disastrous self-will and "hidden sin." Notice that in Hebrews

12:7, hardship and discipline are equated. We need to begin seeing the hardships we go through as God's loving discipline. Allowing hardships, big and small, is how God sanctifies. Allowing hardships is how God frees us more and more experientially from the control of sin that lives in us.

Fénelon wrote: "Whatever light, whatever feeling we may possess, is all a delusion, if it leads us not to the real and constant practice of dying to self."[9] And "It is the continual death of self that constitutes the life of faith."[10] Dying = letting go = just living.

We have previously spoken of how the Holy Spirit who lives inside of us always fills in space created by our letting go. He fills those spaces with Himself. The Christian life is one of continual letting go and being filled (Ephesians 5:18). The Christian life is one of ongoing, ever-deepening dying so that we can be filled up more and more by the indwelling Spirit. Sanctification is the process of God's causing us to let go of control at ever-deepening levels of our being so we can be filled up with Him. It is the process of our loving, faithful Father working in us to free us from ourselves and give us Himself. We must begin to recognize all troubles that come into our lives as God working in us to free us from ourselves and give us Himself. Then we will begin to consider it pure joy whenever we face trials of many kinds (James 1:2). "The fullness of joy is seeing God in all things."[11]

God's Discipline Is an Expression of His Love That Surpasses Knowledge

Dying to self does not need to be a mystery. What I have described in these paragraphs is what it means. Sanctification is the slow, loving process of God causing us to let go of control at ever-deepening levels of our being, and we "learn" this letting go of control through suffering (Philippians 3:10–11). At the level and to the degree we are beginning to understand this is at the level and to the degree we are beginning to understand "this love that surpasses knowledge" (Ephesians 3:19; Job 7:17–19).

God's "love that surpasses knowledge" (Ephesians 3:17–19) begins to be recognized, known, and felt by us when, as, and to the degree we begin to recognize and understand Job 7:17–19 as God's way of constantly, continually working in us to free us from ourselves and give us Himself. He really does pay that much attention to each of us. We will discuss this passage in detail in the next chapter.

Again, please recognize and understand that Job 7:17–19, and the truth that everything is God working in us to further sanctify us, accurately interprets and explains everything that comes into your life and mind down to the tiniest detail, nuance, thought, and feeling. Your loving Father is either causing or permitting everything that comes into your life, both outwardly and inwardly. He really is that attentive to you. He is the perfect Shepherd of your soul. He only lets through what His wisdom allows. "The fullness of joy is seeing God in all things" (Julian of Norwich).[12] Since everything is God working in us to further sanctify us, then He is always intimately close. I trust you are beginning to know this love that surpasses knowledge—that you may be filled to the measure of all the fullness of God (Ephesians 3:19). Recognize and understand God for who He is: "God is love" (1 John 4:16).

We have been predestined to be conformed to the likeness of Jesus. Jesus learned obedience from what He suffered and so do we. He was made "perfect" through testing, and so are we (Job 7:18). It is a testing to see if we will "reverently submit," as He did. It is a testing to see if we will let go of self-will, at whatever level and in whatever form it takes at the time, as He did (Mark 14:35–36).

Hebrews 5:7–10 and Philippians 3:10–11

At the beginning of this chapter on Hebrews 5:7–10, I said this was a key passage in understanding what Paul means by "becoming like Him in His death" in Philippians 3:10. Hebrews 5:7–10 teaches us about and helps us understand Philippians 3:10–11.

Paul wanted to know the fellowship of sharing in Christ's sufferings because suffering along with others, going through what they're going through along with them, is a huge part of getting to know them. Going through what others have gone through, feeling what they have felt, a fellowship of this kind, is how we get to know them. Going through suffering together creates a special bond.

But also, and even more importantly, Paul wanted to experience the fellowship of sharing in Christ's sufferings because this is how, by God's grace, he would learn how to respond to suffering as Christ did, and thereby attain to greater and greater experiential oneness with his Lord. Becoming like Christ in His death was how Paul would become like Him in His life, is how Paul would attain to the resurrection from the dead. Attaining to the resurrection from the dead = becoming Christlike in His life = being conformed to His likeness (Romans 8:29) = becoming "perfect" (Philippians 3:12). Perfection = experiential oneness with Christ in spirit, character, and behavior. Perfection, greater and greater experiential oneness with Christ in this life, comes from losing myself in Him. Losing myself in Him = dying to self = just living.

Becoming like Christ in His death is how, somehow, we attain to the resurrection from the dead. Becoming like Christ in His death is how we attain to greater and more complete experiential oneness with Christ in this life. "Knowing" Christ means greater and greater experiential oneness with Christ in this life. To "know" Christ is to become one with Him experientially. We get this through the fellowship of sharing in His sufferings and becoming like Him in His death in response to these sufferings. For us, becoming like Him in His death = dying to self = letting go of control at ever-deepening levels of our being and just living = "Yet not what I will, but what You will" (Mark 14:36).

Letting go = just living, just living all the time no matter what. Just living = living by faith because the whole and only reason I'm just living is because I'm knowing and believing that Jesus Himself is and will be living through me as I just live.

We won't become "perfect" like Jesus in this life (Philippians 3:12) as long as we are in these bodies with a sin nature (Romans 7:14–25). We won't achieve perfect experiential oneness with the risen Christ in this life, but we can get blissfully, restfully closer than we think by becoming like Him in His death, by learning submission of our will to the will of Another and just living, through suffering.

Several years ago, a popular bumper sticker read, "He who dies with the most toys wins." Every time I saw it, it bugged me. Thankfully I haven't seen one in a long time. At some point, I decided to create my own bumper sticker in response to this one that annoyed me. I had some printed up that read, "He who dies the most before he dies wins." I gave a couple out to some friends and had one on my own car for a while. I offered one to my pastor. He politely declined, saying, "I'm not big on bumper stickers, but if I ever did have one, that's the one I'd have." I must admit I did get a strange sense of pleasure from having that on my car. I really do believe what it says. He who dies the most before he dies wins because he who dies the most gets filled up and lived through the most by Him who lives within us.

— 14 —

His Love That Surpasses Knowledge

JOB 7:17–20

*Children of God—and everyone else—think nobody loves
them enough for them to let go of control.*

—Larry Crabb

We are all familiar with the story of Job. God allowed Satan
to destroy and steal all of Job's flocks and herds and
servants and to kill all his children, all in one day. Job responded
by falling to the ground in worship:

> Naked I came from my mother's womb, and naked I will
> depart. The LORD gave and the LORD has taken away; may
> the name of the LORD be praised. In all this, Job did not sin
> by charging God with wrongdoing. (Job 1:21–22)

After this, God allowed Satan to afflict Job "with painful
sores from the soles of his feet to the top of his head. Then Job
took a piece of broken pottery and scraped himself with it as he
sat among the ashes" (Job 2:7–8). Job's wife, in her great loss,
discouragement, and grief, told Job that it was time to give up and
let go of his "integrity," that he should "curse God and die" (Job

2:9). Job responded, "You are talking like a foolish woman. Shall we accept good from God, and not trouble?" Scripture tells us, "In all this, Job did not sin in what he said." (See Job 2:9–10.)

Not that all this loss came easily to Job. Speaking out of the anguish of his spirit (Job 7:11) he said this: "What is man that you make so much of him, that you give him so much attention, that you examine him every morning and test him every moment? Will you never look away from me, or let me alone even for an instant? If I have sinned, what have I done to you, O watcher of men?" (Job 7:17–20).

In these words, Job is speaking negatively of God making "so much of him," of God giving him "so much attention," of God examining him every morning and testing him every moment, and of God never looking away from him and never letting him alone even for an instant. Job wants God to stop giving him so much attention, to stop examining and testing him. He wants God to look away from him and let him alone.

Eventually, Job's three friends come sit with him and try to explain God to him; these friends are convinced that Job must have done something wrong to deserve all this trouble. After listening to them, Job speaks up to answer his friends' accusations. He intends to defend and vindicate himself, and even challenge God to a showdown in court. Contrary to his friends' assertions, Job is unaware of anything he has done wrong. He believes his heart has been right in all that he has done. He is sure he has committed no willful sin against God.

At the same time, Job is unaware of all that is going on invisibly, behind the scenes, between God and Satan. He is unaware of all that is going on in the spiritual realm. He eventually does challenge and ask God for his "day in court." He insists and counts on his own righteousness as his defense. In the later chapters, God answers Job, and Job replies, "I despise myself and repent in dust and ashes" (Job 42:6). We will look at these things more closely later.

Job Is a Book About Sanctification

We must understand the book of Job as a description of God's work of sanctification in the believer. The book is not *just* about sanctification, but it does include sanctification. It is about God's dealing with and freeing a believer from an area of "sin living in me" (Romans 7:17). Under the great pressure and anguish of the trials, indwelling sin rose to the surface and became visible both to others and eventually to Job. In fact, this book is about God using an unsuspecting devil as an instrument to more completely conform one of His servants to the likeness of Christ. We must understand the book of Job as a model and historical occurrence of sanctification and working of greater holiness in one of His beloved children, as He does with us.

In the beginning of the book, in chapter 1, verse 8, God calls Job "my servant Job" and says of him, "There is no one on earth like him; he is blameless and upright, a man who fears God and shuns evil."

You may then ask, "How can this be a book about sanctification?" God calls Job "blameless and upright, a man who fears God and shuns evil." Yes, but God says the same of us. God says the same of all of His true children, and we are all still being sanctified, especially of sin living in us. Understanding sanctification as God dealing with and freeing us from the control of sin living in us makes sense of the book of Job, and of our own lives. Everything every moment is God working in us to free us from ourselves and give us Himself.

The book of Job is about sanctification. Job indeed is "blameless and upright." God Himself calls him righteous. Job is righteous for the same reason we are . . . by grace through faith. Job was justified by his faith, just as we are. Job feared God and shunned evil. We are justified by faith, and we still go through sanctification and the process of being made "perfect" (Philippians 3:12). We still go through the process of being conformed to the likeness of

His Son, just as Job did. And it happened through suffering. It took suffering to cause sin that lived in him to come to the surface and be exposed so that Job could repent, so that he could let go of control and pride at an even deeper level than he had before. And God is doing the same with us. Most of us certainly do not go through trial and trouble at the level and to the degree that Job did, but we do go through it, and for the same reason as Job.

So, yes, God calls Job (already) righteous and, in this book, God is and would be, until Job left his earthly body, continually working in Job to cause him to let go of control and pride at ever-deepening levels of his being. And God does the same with us. We are already righteous, by grace through faith, and God is and will be, until we leave these bodies of ours, continually working in us to cause us to let go of control at ever-deepening levels of our being, because He chooses to, because we have been predestined to be conformed to the likeness of His Son. The book of Job and our lives as Christians are true stories of intimate purgation.

Hidden Works of Self-Love

In chapters 1 and 2, as we have said, the Holy Spirit makes a point of stating three times that Job was "blameless and upright; a man who fears God and shuns evil" (Job 1:8). We too, by grace through faith, are "holy and blameless in His sight," now and forever (Ephesians 1:4–8). In all the experience of his initial trial, the loss of all his possessions and children, "Job did not sin by charging God with wrongdoing" (Job 1:22). In response to his second test, the loss of health, "Job did not sin in what he said" (2:10).

As we said earlier, in 7:17–19, Job saw God's intense attention as negative. He saw God as making too much of him, as giving him too much attention. He didn't like God's examining him every morning and testing him every moment, never looking away or leaving him alone. In other words, Job wanted God to focus His attention on someone else for a change.

129

In verses 20–21 of chapter 7, Job says, "If I have sinned, what have I done to you, O watcher of men? Why have you made me your target? Have I become a burden to you? Why do you not pardon my offenses and forgive my sins?" Had God's response to this question been recorded, I believe it would read, "I have. Pardon and forgiveness are not what this is about."

As with Job, as God makes hidden sin more apparent, we repent and surrender to Him more deeply.

Job was unaware of any willful sin in his life. If he had been aware of some sin, he surely would have confessed and offered sacrifice, as he did for his children every morning (1:5). Job does not and cannot see the sin that God is dealing with because it is "sin living in him" that God is dealing with through the testing.

Fénelon said, "You must learn to act calmly and in continual dependence on the Spirit of grace, mortifying all the *hidden* works of self-love."[1] We cannot mortify hidden works of self-love ourselves, because they're hidden. It is God the Holy Spirit who does this work as we persevere and lean not on our own understanding (Proverbs 3:5). According to Fénelon, the way we mortify the hidden works of self-love is by calm, continual dependence on the Spirit of grace (Galatians 5:16). As with Job, as God makes hidden sin more apparent, we repent and surrender to Him more deeply. (See Job 40–42:6.)

We mortify the hidden works of self-love by saying, and meaning it, "Yet not what I will, but what You will" in the midst of suffering that makes no sense and tempts us to doubt God's love (Mark 14:36). We mortify the hidden works of self-love by trusting God anyway, because something is going on behind the scenes of which we know nothing, and we trust that it is good.

Job's Sin That Lived in Him (Romans 7:17–20)

Job says, "*If* I have sinned . . ." (7:20, emphasis mine). He is trying to understand why he is going through what he is going through. He is confused. His suffering doesn't make sense to his logical mind or according to the reasoning of the day—that is, the "just world" view that God rewards the righteous and punishes the wicked. Job honestly doesn't know of anything he has done wrong, so he is greatly confused and ends up insisting on an answer. He comes to the place of insisting on understanding. He comes to the place of limiting God to the confines of his comparatively puny created mind. This, of course, is a component of the indwelling sin of pride that comes to the surface under the extreme duress of his trials.

Sanctification has to do with freeing us from "sin living in me," sin that is initially, and sometimes indefinitely, unknown to us and known only to God. It is already forgiven, but it's getting in the way of knowing God more intimately, and He is dealing with it. "Sin living in me" can also be sin that we do know about and recognize, but we just can't stop doing it. Job's case was the former.

For Job, indwelling sin took the form of pridefully limiting God to the confines of his finite created mind. Sin took the form of insisting on knowing what he could not understand versus fully trusting God and humbling himself under God's mighty hand in the midst of confusion and not understanding. Job's trust had to be in God Himself versus his own understanding. Job was guilty of "leaning on his own understanding" versus trusting in God "with all his heart." Interestingly, Job's sin and Asaph's in Psalm 73 are fundamentally the same.

When we trust in God with *all* our heart, there is no room for us to be doing anything contrary to that in our heart. When we trust in God with all our mind, there is no room for us to be doing anything contrary to that in our mind. The only way we can trust in God this way is "by the Spirit" (Romans 8:12–14). Also see the Romans 6 diagram on p. 49.

Job was falling short in a way that we all do: indwelling sin in the form of not fully trusting God in the context of going through trial and suffering of which Job couldn't make sense, as well as in the context of something important going on in the spiritual realm of which Job had no idea. Job needed to learn obedience in the form of reverently submitting to the fact of Isaiah 55:8–9: " 'For my thoughts are not your thoughts, neither are your ways my ways,' declares the LORD. 'As the heavens are higher than the earth, so are my ways higher than your ways and my thoughts than your thoughts.' "

Thus God speaks to Job in chapter 38:

> Who is this that darkens my counsel with words without knowledge? Brace yourself like a man; I will question you, and you shall answer me. Where were you when I laid the earth's foundation? Tell me, if you understand, who marked off its dimensions? Surely you know! Who stretched a measuring line across it? . . . Have you comprehended the vast expanses of the earth? Tell me, if you know all this. What is the way to the abode of light? And where does darkness reside? . . . Surely you know, for you were already born! You have lived so many years! (Job 38:2–5,18–19,21)

But all this sin was not something Job could initially see or understand as going on in himself. Job's sins were "hidden faults." He says, "*If* I have sinned, what I have I done to you, O watcher of men?" (7:20, emphasis mine). And God eventually shows him.

God is holy. Jesus learned obedience from what He suffered, and so do we. Being conformed to the likeness of Christ is hard and sometimes agonizing. Each of us must answer the question for ourselves, "How badly do I want it?" (See Romans 8:28–29; Philippians 3:10–11; Job 42:5.)

Two Kinds of Sin

Scripture speaks of "hidden" sin and "willful" sin in Psalm 19:12–13: "Who can discern his errors [that is, his *own* errors]? Forgive my hidden faults. Keep your servant also from willful sins; may they not rule over me. Then will I be blameless, innocent of great transgression."

Under the heat of suffering, Job's "hidden faults" surface and become evident. When God confronts Job through hard questioning in the later chapters, Job "sees" and repents. These "hidden faults" are comparable to what Paul calls "sin living in me," rooted in the sinful nature. "Seeing" this sin does not come from intense introspection or constant self-examination. Seeing comes only from God, in His perfect way, in His perfect timing, through His inner work of sanctification as we just live, counting ourselves dead to the penalty and controlling power of sin but alive to God in Christ Jesus. And even then, it is not guaranteed that we will see or understand all of what is going on inside of us. But we will see enough to be able to repent, to be able to let go, to be able to surrender and stop insisting on our own understanding and control.

Of course, just as we're already forgiven for willful sin, so we're already forgiven for sin that lives in us. Sanctification is not a matter of pardon and forgiveness. We already have that. Sanctification is the process of God freeing us from sin more and more experientially as part of His work in conforming us to the likeness of Christ. Sanctification is an expression of God's "love that surpasses knowledge" (Ephesians 3:19).

"Sin That Lives in Me" Is Rooted in the Sin Nature

For much of the book, Job argues with his friends, complains out of the bitterness of his soul, gets angry, and ends up challenging God to a courtroom showdown. Indwelling sin, that has existed in

Job from the moment he was conceived (see Psalm 51:5), comes to the surface in the context of the intense "heat" of suffering. This is important. This indwelling sin was always there. It was not created by the circumstances or his friends' false analyses of the problem and accusations. Circumstances and other people only serve to bring out the sin that is already there. It's just that only God can see it. And, therefore, only God can deal with this indwelling sin in His perfect way, in His perfect timing. And He does, and He is, as we just live. God working in us this way is part of His work in transforming us into Christ's likeness with ever-increasing glory, which comes from the Lord, who is the Spirit (2 Corinthians 3:18).

Our Inward Struggling Is Struggling Against God

Our Father's dealing with indwelling sin that is hidden from us interprets and explains most, if not all, of our times of inward struggle and discontent. In reality, when we are struggling inwardly, we are struggling with God for control (Galatians 5:16–18). Thankfully, God always wins, in His perfect timing, in His perfect way. We can know that our times of inward struggle and discontent are actually struggling with God, as Job was, because God is continually making much of us and giving us much attention. He is examining us every morning and testing us every moment. He never looks away from us or lets us alone even for an instant. Times of inward struggle are times when God is working in us to let go of control and trust Him at a newer, deeper level than before. Likewise, we come out of it letting go, trusting Him, and just living at a newer, deeper level than before (2 Corinthians 4:10–11).

Everything every moment is God working in us to free us from ourselves (our self, the self, the self-life) and give us Himself. Everything every moment is God working in us to free us more and more experientially from the sin nature and give us Himself more and more experientially. This is what He was doing with Job: "My ears had heard of you but now my eyes have seen you. Therefore I despise myself and repent in dust and ashes" (Job 42:5–6). Job recognized his sin of accusing God. In light of "seeing" God more clearly, he saw his pridefulness more clearly and was appalled by it.

Because everything is God working in us to cause us to let go of control at ever-deepening levels of our being, inward struggling is always struggling with Him. In other words, if we were perfectly trusting in Him, then we would be perfectly resting in Him, all the time, no matter what. If I'm inwardly struggling for control in some form at some level, then I'm not perfectly resting, which means I'm not perfectly trusting. I'm not "letting go." This is why John Owen said, "Resting in Him as [my] utmost end."[2] Resting in Him = just living = living by the Spirit.

It's All God

God's love is such that everything every moment is Him working in us to free us from ourselves and give us Himself. It will be very helpful and significant, regarding our spiritual advancement, when we begin to recognize and accept this fact. He is the perfect Shepherd of our soul. He lets through what He lets through, both outwardly and inwardly, for our good and His glory, for our sanctification and thereby for His glory, that others may be drawn to Him through us. God's desire is to show Himself holy through us as we just live, and He does and He will continue to do so.

Let's consider two prayers from the book of Psalms:

> Search me, O God, and know my heart; test me and know my anxious thoughts. See if there is any offensive way in me, and lead me in the way everlasting. (Psalm 139:23–24)

Direct my footsteps according to your word; let no sin rule over me. (Psalm 119:133)

We can count on these words being true for us as we just live. We can rejoice in the fact that God is and will be directing our footsteps according to His Word, and He is and will be letting no sin rule over us as we just live. God's letting no sin rule over me is a perfect description of His ongoing, moment-by-moment working in me to free me from myself, to free me more and more experientially from the sin nature, and to give me Himself = progressive sanctification = attaining to the resurrection from the dead (Philippians 3:11). Sanctification is the process of the oneness with our resurrected Lord, that we already have, becoming more and more real in our experience by grace through faith as we just live.

In the midst of the inward struggle, which is really a struggle for control (Galatians 5:16–18), our part is to die, to let go of control at this new level within us at which God is now working. In other words, our part in this agonizing inward battle for control between the sinful nature and the Spirit is becoming like Him in His death (Mark 14:35–36; Hebrews 5:7–10) and thereby gradually attaining to the resurrection from the dead = experiential oneness with Christ with whom we are already one.

It is for God to show us what we need to see as we just live. Pray the above Psalm 139 and 119 verses for yourself, count on them being so, leave it in His hands and just live. We are not to be thinking about our sin. We have been freed from it. We are to be just living (Romans 6:11) because we believe that we are one with Him now and that He will be living through us as we just live. It is His will and purpose and love and plan for you to deal with you and your sin that lives in you, because He chooses to. So you need not be surprised, confused, or bewildered when things happen, when outward and inward trials come. It's Him. It's all

Him. It's Him working in you to free you from yourself; it's His love that surpasses knowledge.

It is only for you to humble yourself under God's mighty hand that He may lift you up in due time. Cast your anxiety on Him because He cares for you and takes care of you. Resist the devil by standing firm in the faith . . . you're not alone in whatever you're going through. And the God of all grace, who called you to His eternal glory in Christ,

> *It is worth it to go through the inward battle caused by outward circumstances.*

after you have suffered a little while, will Himself restore you and make you strong, firm and steadfast, just as He did with Job. (See 1 Peter 5:6–11.)

God Answers Job

Finally God responds to Job beginning in chapter 38: "Who is this that darkens my counsel with words without knowledge? Brace yourself like a man; I will question you, and you shall answer me. Where were you when I laid the earth's foundation? Tell me, if you understand. Who marked off its dimensions? Surely you know!" (vv. 2–5). The Lord's sarcasm is very evident.

The Lord continues in 38:19–21, "What is the way to the abode of light? And where does darkness reside? Can you take them to their places? Do you know the paths to their dwellings? Surely you know, for you were already born! You have lived so many years!"

Of course, God is in this way confronting Job with his pride, with his judging God according to the limits of his own finite created mind. God is beginning to show Job the "sin living in him" that was controlling Job and limiting his further spiritual growth, without Job even being aware of it. Only God knew of this sin dwelling in Job, and only God could free him from it, and this freeing him came through suffering. So it is with us. "It is the fire of suffering that brings forth the gold of godliness," wrote Jeanne Guyon.[3]

God continues to show Job his indwelling sin through His word, through questioning Job rhetorically and showing him his pride. Finally God says to Job in chapter 40:2, "Will the one who contends with the Almighty correct him? Let him who accuses God answer him!"

Job Answers God

Job answers, "I am unworthy—how can I reply to you? I put my hand over my mouth. I spoke once, but I have no answer— twice, but I will say no more" (40:4–5).

God has more revealing questions for Job in the rest of chapter 40 and into 41. Lastly, in chapter 42:2–5, Job says:

> I know that you can do all things; no plan of yours can be thwarted. You asked, "Who is this that obscures my counsel without knowledge?" Surely I spoke of things I did not understand, things too wonderful for me to know. You said, "Listen now, and I will speak; I will question you, and you shall answer me." My ears had heard of you but now my eyes have seen you. Therefore I despise myself and repent in dust and ashes.

Job repents. This book is about sanctification. This book is about God lovingly, firmly working within Job through the inward effects of suffering to free Job from himself and give Job more of Himself. The same is true for us. This book is written for us.

Job and 1 Peter 5:10–11

What Job learned, and what we can learn too, is that it is worth it to go through the inward battle caused by the outward (or inward) circumstances. Consider this passage from Job 42: "After Job had prayed for his friends, the LORD made him prosperous again and gave him twice as much as he had before [cf. 1 Peter 5:10, 11]. All his brothers and sisters and everyone who had known him before came and ate with him in his house. They comforted and consoled him over all the trouble the LORD had brought upon him, and each one gave him a piece of silver and a gold ring. The LORD blessed the latter part of Job's life more than the first" (vv. 10–12).

We must also see that, more importantly, after his trial and testing, Job had a deeper, more intimate knowledge and fear of God: "My ears had heard of you but now my eyes have seen you. Therefore I despise myself and repent in dust and ashes" (vv. 5–6).

This is how God works in our lives to free us from ourselves and to give us Himself, to free us more and more experientially from sin that lives in us (the sinful nature) and to give us Himself more and more experientially/intimately. "I want to know Christ" (Philippians 3:10). We learn obedience from what we suffer. We learn letting go; we learn dying to self; and we learn just living from what we suffer.

For the Christian walking with the Lord, for the Christian living by the Spirit, trials and troubles, hardships and God's discipline are all for the purpose of freeing us from sin living in us—the "sin living in me" that Paul speaks of in Romans 7:17, 20—that may be unknown to us, yet sometimes still controlling us at some level. God's loving sanctification—our Father's continual working in us and on us to free us from ourselves and give us Himself—accurately interprets and explains all that we go through, both outwardly and inwardly, down to the tiniest details and nuances of our outward and inward experiences. Remember Job 7:17–19 and intimate purgation.

"Will you never look away from me, or let me alone, even for an instant?" God would answer us, "No, I love you too much. I want all of you too much, and I want you to have all of me too much."

Oh, Father, Son, Holy Spirit, thank you. The fullness of joy is seeing You in all things.[4]

Again, because he had only "heard of" the Lord, 42:5, because he had only limited knowledge of Him and His ways, Job had seen God's trials and testing as only negative and punishing, even seeing it as unjust punishing, as God making a mistake. In 7:17–19, the Lord's making so much of him, giving him so much attention, examining him every morning and testing him every moment, never looking away from him or leaving him alone even for an instant were all being falsely interpreted and expressed by Job as negative and punishing. We must not commit the same error.

In 42:5–6, Job says, "My ears had heard of you but now my eyes have seen you. Therefore I despise myself and repent in dust and ashes." With greater knowledge of God came great repentance and great humility. There came a drastic shift from accusing God and "speaking of things he did not understand" to heartfelt repenting and self-lowering (cf. 1 Peter 5:6–9). There was now a much greater and deeper fear of the Lord. Great, deeply rooted foolishness was replaced by great, deeply rooted fear of the Lord and a sincere and heartfelt knowledge that God knew more than Job did.

What a wonderful, blessed thing God had done in Job's life. He had freed Job from an area of deeply rooted pride and self-life and replaced it with a deeply rooted humility and knowledge of Himself. And it happened through suffering. God's making Job prosperous again, giving him twice as much as he had before and blessing the latter part of his life more than the first (42:10–12), were just icing on the cake. As a result of suffering, Job knew God more intimately than before. Again, compare Philippians 3:10–11: "I want to know Christ and the power of his resurrection and the fellowship of sharing in his sufferings, becoming like him in his death, and so, somehow, to attain to the resurrection from the dead."

Knowing Christ really is the best thing there is. It is treasure hidden in a field. Christ Himself and knowing Him intimately through sharing in His sufferings are the real "treasures of darkness, riches stored in secret places" that Isaiah speaks of in Isaiah 45:3.

Personalize Job 7:17–19 and Recognize That Everything Is God Working in You

From the book of Job, we learn a life-changing lesson. We learn that Job 7:17–19 contains good and blessed truths. We need to read and pray these verses with this attitude: "Who am I that You make so much of me, that You give me so much attention, that You examine me every morning and test me every moment? Will You never look away from me or let me alone even for an instant?"

And then hear God's answer to this question: "No, never and not even for an instant. Every moment, no matter what the moment is, finds Me working in you to free you from yourself and give you Myself. My deepest desire is to fully give Myself to you. This is my love for you that surpasses knowledge. You can trust Me."

In other words, if God is examining you every morning and testing you every moment and never looks away from you or leaves you alone even for an instant, doesn't this explain everything going on inside of you every moment? God is always intimately close. He is either causing or permitting everything that comes into your life and mind, for your good and His purposes and glory. In everything, God is working in you to free you more and more from self experientially and give you more and more of Himself, experientially. Yes, He is making that much of you . . . He is giving you that much attention . . . He *is* that good.

Ultimately, God's testing is to see if you'll die, if you'll simply let go to Him and His will, if you'll become like Him in His death (Mark 14:35-36). The testing is to cause you to let go of control in whatever way and at whatever level you're currently holding onto it. All letting go is letting go to God because He lives in you and He always fills in space created by brokenness with Himself. He doesn't tempt you, but certainly He allows you to be tempted. He allows you to be tempted, just as He did with Jesus and with Job: by the world, the worldly, the sinful nature, and the devil. His grace is sufficient for you in those moments to enable you to trust Him to fill you and thereby enable you to make right choices (Romans 8:12–14).

Another kind of testing has to do with those "everyday critical moments." God allows us to be tempted in our minds. Throughout the day, we can be bombarded and tormented by all kinds of thoughts and desires. He allows us to be tempted in our vision and encounters with others. The fruit of the Spirit is . . . self-control. We choose in those moments where to direct our eyes, our minds, and ourselves.

Your loving Father's attention to you is constant. Every moment is Him, no matter what the moment is, no matter what this moment right now is as you're reading this. As you're reading this, He is working deep inside of you because, as Job 7:17–19 tells us, He is continually working inside of us. Everything is Him working in you to free you from yourself and give you Himself. Whatever you're feeling inside of yourself right now, no matter what it is, is God working in you to cause you to let go of control at a deeper level than you have before. Whatever is going on inside of you right now is God working in you, freeing you from yourself and giving you Himself. This is His love that surpasses knowledge (Ephesians 3:14–19).

The Inward Battle in a Nutshell

Sanctification regarding indwelling sin takes time. What we want in our spirit more than anything, our flesh (the sin nature) fights against just as hard. This is the Galatians 5:16–18 inward struggle. This is the Romans 7:14–25 inward struggle. The answer is the same in both passages . . . letting go to the indwelling, filling, controlling, more-powerful-than-the-sin-nature Holy Spirit = just letting go because He already lives in you and is controlling you = just living (Galatians 5:16–18; Romans 8:1–4, 9).

The reason we struggle is that we're resisting Him taking us deeper through suffering. Many times, in the case of inward struggle and suffering, we cause our own pain by resisting letting go of control (Psalm 73:16). The way to freedom from sin is living by the Spirit = just living because we're already controlled by Him (Romans 8:9). In other words, the way to freedom from sin and inward struggle is letting go of control at whatever level and in whatever form control is happening. We will recognize it when we're doing it, and we do it often. But we'll be doing it less and less as we grow in faith through the experience of intimate purgation.

There Is Only Pain Where There's Still Life

God's "examining" us (Job 7:18) is to see where there's still life, where there is still self-life, to see where we still need to die, to see where we still need to let go of control. Fénelon said, "There is only pain where there's still life." Of course, God already knows this. He doesn't find out something about us in the morning that He didn't already know from eternity past. This is poetic language, and it is still good and right to think of God as examining us every morning, just as His compassions "never fail" and "are new every morning" (Lamentations 3:22–23).

As I said, He examines us to see where there is still self-life. His testing us every moment is not to see if we can figure out what it is we're doing wrong or not doing right, and then if we can discover this and correct it, things will start going well for us again. This testing is not to make sure that we're "getting it right," that we're performing correctly in all the ways that we should be. This testing is to see if we'll die so He can fill us up. This testing is to see if we'll let go of control, if we'll die, if we'll surrender at this new mysterious level at which God is dealing with us. It is a testing to see if we'll die to self, not to see if we'll try harder or correct ourselves or finally get it right in some area we keep failing in. It is a testing to see if we'll die—if, by God's stronger grace, we'll let go of control at a level deeper than we have before = sanctification. It is a testing to see if we'll become like Him in His death, in response to the fellowship of sharing in His sufferings. And we will, eventually, no matter how hard we initially fight against it. As A. W. Tozer said, "The cross . . . always has its way."[5]

In Romans 7:24–25, the apostle Paul proclaimed, "What a wretched man I am! Who will rescue me from this body of death? Thanks be to God—through Jesus Christ our Lord!"

The "body of death" is not our physical body. The body of death to which Paul refers is our sin nature, which we will have as long as we are in these physical bodies. God Himself rescues us and frees us more and more experientially from the sinful nature's power as we live by the Spirit though faith, as we put to death the misdeeds of the body by the Spirit (Romans 8:13).

This is good news for those of us who are being tempted to hate ourselves and give up because of continual failure. Do not hate yourself; humble yourself. Do not waste time hating yourself and beating yourself up for sinning. Jesus was already hated and beaten up for you, in your place. As a child of God, you're forgiven, even when you behave like a brute beast before Him (Psalm 73:21–24).

St. Augustine summed it up well: "We must be made to feel our weakness, our wretchedness, our inability to correct ourselves. We must give up hope in ourselves and have no hope but in God."

The "Real and Constant Practice of Dying to Self"

Consider these words of Fénelon: "Whatever light, whatever feeling we may possess, is all a delusion, if it lead us not to the real and constant practice of dying to self."[6]

Dying to self is an inward, deeply personal, and individual thing. There are "hidden faults," "offensive ways," and deep, inner selfish movements and patterns that are harmful to ourselves and others that we must be freed from, that we must let go of, that only God knows about. This explains much of our inward discomfort and agitation.

Your loving Father never looks away from you or leaves you alone, even for an instant. This is a good thing! Job didn't mean for God to leave him all alone, depart from him. Job meant, "Will you never stop troubling me? Give me a break already. You don't even let me sleep (vv. 13–14). If I have sinned, show me and then I can fix it!" (v. 20).

He never takes His eye off you. He is always attentive. He is always working in you to free you from yourself and give you Himself. He is always working in you to free you from yourself at the next level. You must see how this explains all your trouble, inward struggles, hardships, and suffering. The inward struggles happen because you are fighting against the Holy Spirit without even knowing it.

Nothing happens apart from God. If nothing happens apart from God, then everything is God working in you to transform you. He's not only close when you feel good and things are going well. He is directly causing or permitting everything that is happening in your life, outwardly and inwardly, for His loving purpose of freeing you from sin and filling in that space created by brokenness, created by finally letting go, with Himself. This is what's going on. This is His work of sanctification. You need look no further regarding why you go through hardships and inner struggles. It's God. You struggle inwardly until you finally give in and give up, until you finally let go. As disciples of Jesus, we learn obedience from what we suffer. We learn reverent submission from what we suffer. We learn dying to self from what we suffer. We learn letting go from what we suffer. We learn just living from what we suffer.

Again, what we want in our spirit more than anything—the inward peace that comes from just letting go—our flesh, the sinful nature, fights against just as hard. The good news is that no matter how hard we fight or for how long, we will eventually let go. God is faithful. He is a good dad. His love is unfailing, doing in us, for us, and through us what He has predetermined for each of us before the creation of the world. He won't let us hold onto control and remain miserable indefinitely. The cross always gets its way. We have been predestined to be conformed to the likeness of His Son. What God predestines, He does. Look no further than these things to interpret and explain all you go through, outwardly and inwardly.

A Clarification About "Yourself"

I feel the need to clarify. When I use the word *yourself* in the sense that everything every moment is God working in you to free you from yourself and give you Himself, I'm using the term *yourself* subjectively. I'm using it in the sense of how we tend to experience ourselves in the midst of the inward battle, as we learn and grow in living by the Spirit through faith.

Romans 6–8 (which, again, we will look at more closely in volume 2) clearly teaches that who and what we actually, factually *are* now is one with Christ, free from sin, controlled by the Spirit, and thereby free to just live. We have a new nature which is Christ

Himself living in us and ruling there. We died to sin and are raised up with Christ. We are in Him, and He is in us.

By the terms *self, yourself, myself,* or *ourselves* in the definition of sanctification, I mean the self in terms of the sin nature, not who we actually, factually are now. The sin nature is real, and we experience it at work in the members of our bodies, and we obey it sometimes, but it is not who and what we *are* now. God freeing me from myself and giving me Himself is God freeing me more and more from the sin nature *experientially* and filling me up with Himself more and more *experientially* as I believe the Scriptures about myself and thereby just live and by the Spirit exercise self-control. Sanctification is the process of God, by grace through faith, making me experientially who I already am, actually and factually. Sanctification is God bringing us to the place of knowing our oneness with Christ and therefore just living. This is a major working in us and in our lives of God's love that surpasses knowledge.

More About God's Love That Surpasses Knowledge

And I pray that you, being rooted and established in love, may have power, together with all the saints, to grasp how wide and long and high and deep is the love of Christ, and to know this love that surpasses knowledge—that you may be filled to the measure of all the fullness of God.

(Ephesians 3:17–19)

God's love that surpasses knowledge is the fact that He makes so very much of you. He gives you constant attention. He examines you every morning and tests you every moment to see if you'll surrender at this next level so you can become more and more free (John 8:32, 36). He never looks away from you, and He will never leave you alone. His working in you to free you from yourself and give you Him is constant. His working in you to free you from yourself and give you Him is every instant (Job 7:19) and therefore explains everything going on in your life, both outwardly and inwardly.

No wonder we are to be "always giving thanks to God the Father for *everything*, in the name of our Lord Jesus Christ" (Ephesians 5:20, emphasis mine). Because in everything every moment, He is working in you to free you from yourself and give you Himself. Oh, Dad, Lord, Holy Spirit, certainly, certainly, certainly the fullness of joy is seeing You in all things.[7]

God Testing Us Every Moment and the Thought Life

God either causes or allows every thought that comes into your mind. He does not tempt you, and He is not the author of evil thoughts. "When tempted, no one should say, 'God is tempting me.' For God cannot be tempted by evil, nor does he tempt anyone; but each one is tempted when, by his own evil desire, he is dragged away and enticed" (James 1:13–14). God does not tempt us, but He does allow us to be tempted. He did with Jesus, and He does with us. (See Luke 4:1–13; Hebrews 4:14–16; 1 Corinthians 10:11–13.)

Sinful, blasphemous, lustful, perverse thoughts and temptations do not come from God. He is not the source of them. They come from our own sinful nature, often with Satan or one of his "messengers" (2 Corinthians 12:7) helping out or directly inserting them. Messengers deliver messages.

But obviously God is allowing this to happen, and not without reason. Fénelon said we should "receive everything that God presents to your mind, notwithstanding the shrinking of nature, as a trial by which He would exercise and strengthen your faith."[8] God is in control of everything that comes into our mind, and the testing of our faith at that point is what we do with whatever is coming into our mind. By the Spirit we can "put to death" these "misdeeds of the body" (Romans 8:13) which in this case affects our thought life, or we can give in to the temptation and entertain the thought and eventually act on it (James 1:15). This is what Fénelon is saying in the above quote. This kind of testing, through our thought life, is how our faith is exercised and strengthened, day by day, moment by moment. When I am out and about, the mental warfare is constant.

Again, it is only by living by the Spirit that we pass the test, that we successfully put to death this misdeed of the body, that we are able to successfully avoid entertaining evil or doubting thoughts, that we successfully "don't go down that road" in our mind.

As Martin Luther put it, "You can't keep the birds from flying over your head, but you can keep them from making a nest in your hair."

And Paul tells us in Romans 8:6, "The mind of sinful man is death, but the mind controlled by the Spirit is life and peace." The key to a growing freedom from giving in to sinful thoughts, the key to being able to not let them make a nest in our hair, is living by the Spirit through faith. It is the same key that is for everything else in the Christian life. Sons and daughters of God are those who, by the Spirit, are continually putting to death the misdeeds of the body.

Suffering Brings Us to the Place of Letting Go and Just Living

As we come to understand the role of suffering in God's work of sanctification, we can begin to understand and be able to say along with Paul, "I want to know Christ and the power of his resurrection and the fellowship of sharing in his sufferings, becoming like him in his death, and so, somehow, to attain to the resurrection from the dead" (Philippians 3:10–11).

Suffering is a vital part of coming to know Christ and the joy, freedom, and peace that come from knowing the reality of actual experiential oneness with Him in this life. Experiential oneness with Christ, and the joy, freedom, rest, and fruitfulness that come along with it, come from the fellowship of sharing in His sufferings and, in response, becoming like Him in His death = dying to self = reverent submission = just living so Christ living in us can be filling us and living through us.

Well-meaning, well-intentioned Christians who are still somewhat confident in themselves think and talk in terms of "living for Jesus." Disciples know better and think and talk in terms of dying for Jesus so He can live through them, because they know He *will* be living through them as they just live. This is because they believe that they no longer live, but Christ lives in them. Dying = just living = living by the Spirit through faith = just living because He already controls you = "free indeed" = wholeness. Just living because He already controls you = just living because you no longer live, but He lives in you = wholeness = where God is bringing us. The pressure's off. In the Christian life, the only pressure we feel is the pressure we put on ourselves due to unbelief and desire for control.

In the words of Larry Crabb with which we started this chapter: "Children of God—and everyone else—think nobody loves them enough for them to let go of control."[9] Or alternately, perhaps: "Children of God—and everyone else—think nobody loves them enough for them to just live."

– 15 –

Press On . . . in What?

PHILIPPIANS 3:12–14

Something or other the soul will be hungering and
thirsting after; therefore they are blessed who fasten
upon the right object.

—Matthew Henry

Let's consider the words of Paul in Philippians 3:12–14: "Not that I have already obtained all this, or have already been made perfect, but I press on to take hold of that for which Christ Jesus took hold of me. Brothers, I do not consider myself yet to have taken hold of it. But one thing I do: Forgetting what is behind and straining toward what is ahead, I press on toward the goal to win the prize for which God has called me heavenward in Christ Jesus."

We do not obtain perfection; we do not obtain complete experiential oneness with the risen, ascended Christ Jesus in this life. As long as we are in these bodies, we have an indwelling still-alive-and-well sin nature that gives us trouble and to which we sometimes still surrender. However, as I said earlier, we can get a whole lot closer to this perfection; we can get a whole lot closer to this complete experiential oneness with Christ Jesus in this life, than we've been led to believe. It is through coming to know and count upon this oneness with Christ that we already have. (See 1 Corinthians 2:12.)

It is by "becoming like Him in His death" in response to experiencing the fellowship of sharing in His sufferings. This is how we "attain to the resurrection from the dead"; this is how the oneness with Christ that we already actually, factually have becomes more and more real in our experience. It is only by dying that we give the risen indwelling Christ, in the person of the Holy Spirit, the opportunity and freedom to control and live through us. Dying = just living.

"Christ came . . . not to get us doing, but to bring us to an undoing," wrote L. E. Maxwell in *Born Crucified*.[1] I would also put it this way: Christ came not to get us doing but to bring us to just living so He could live through us.

Paul Presses On in Wanting to Attain to Perfect Experiential Oneness with Christ

Paul says he "presses on." What does he press on in? He presses on in wanting to know Christ and the power of His resurrection and the fellowship of sharing in His sufferings. How does he respond to sharing in Christ's sufferings in such a way that it leads to attaining to the resurrection from the dead? How does Paul respond to experiencing Christ's sufferings in such a way as to lead to greater and greater experiential oneness with Christ in this life, while living in this world? How does Paul respond to sharing in Christ's sufferings in such a way as to become as Christlike as possible while living in his body in this world? Paul responds to sharing in Christ's sufferings by becoming like Him in His death. Paul presses on in becoming like Christ in His death when going through outward and inward suffering. Paul presses on in dying to self. In the face of suffering, Paul presses on in letting go of control and self-will at ever-deepening levels of his being so that Christ can more and more freely live through him. Paul presses on in the faith that believes this. Paul presses on in the faith that utterly depends on and counts on nothing but his oneness with the risen Christ Jesus Himself, for everything.

You see, Paul does want to become "perfect." He does want to become as complete and whole and Christlike in this world as one possibly can. He does want to attain to the resurrection from the dead = he does want the oneness he already actually, factually has with Christ to become as real as possible in his experience while in this body in this world because he knows this is how Christ will most effectively do the work of winning the world. The New Covenant of the Spirit is the truth that God's way of winning the world is by literally living through His people (Ezekiel 36:22–23, 26–27; John 15:5).

J. D. G. Dunn said, "Religious experience for Paul is basically experience of union with Christ."[2] This is where God is bringing us. Experiential union with Christ = wholeness.

Paul Wants to Win

Paul wants nothing less than to be "perfect," to be complete, to attain to perfect experiential oneness with his risen Lord. This is his "goal." In fact, he says he wants to "win the prize"; he wants to come in first; he wants to be the best and most Christlike while living in this world (Philippians 3:14; 1 Corinthians 9:24). How? By the fellowship of sharing in Christ's sufferings and in response to these sufferings becoming like Christ in His death. And so, somehow, this way, by dying, attaining to the resurrection from the dead = attaining to perfection = attaining to the greatest degree of experiential oneness with Christ possible in this life. Paul wants to win . . . he wants to be best at this.

He who dies the most before he dies wins. This is because the one who dies the most is the one who will have Christ living through him or her the most. Dying = just living = living by the Spirit = abiding in the Vine = Christ living through us = bearing much fruit = winning the prize.

Paul is not satisfied with a Romans 7:14–25 Christian life—a life that doesn't get any better than a continual bondage to sin, a life that is merely an ongoing cycle of continual failure and confession, and it doesn't get any better than that. Failure is accepted . . . resignation to its inevitable rule and confessing when it happens is as good as it gets. This is not Paul's gospel.

Like Paul, we all want to be perfect. Deep inside, we want perfection more than anything. Also, if we're willing to admit it, we each want to win; we each want to be the best. What is crucial is wanting to be best at the right thing.

It Is Good to Want to Win

It is normal to want to be whole, increasingly sinless, free, and joyful. How do we get there? How do we attain to the resurrection from the dead more and more in this life? It has to do with how we respond to the fellowship of sharing in Christ's sufferings. As stated above, it has to do with the last thing Paul says that we are to be pressing on in, which is "becoming like Him in His death."

We each want to be the best. But the only thing that really matters, as far as being the best at Christlikeness, is being the best at dying = being the best at just living so Christ can live through us. He who dies the most before he dies wins. The one who is best at just living is the one who believes the most that he no longer lives but Christ lives in him and will be living through him as he just lives.

I want to be the best at dying so I can win, so I can be the most Christlike. I confess . . . I want to win at this. I'm okay with this because Paul says that's the way we are to "run" so that we may win. "Do you not know that in a race all the runners run, but only one gets the prize? Run in such a way as to get the prize" (1 Corinthians 9:24).

It isn't a matter of comparing ourselves to one other. Don't waste time doing that. Don't look to the left or to the right. We fix our eyes on Jesus, the author and perfecter of our faith (Hebrews

12:2), not on each other and not on ourselves. Jesus is the perfecter of my faith, not any other person and not me. Wanting to win certainly isn't a matter of pride. Because the way we become the best is by dying—by dying to self, by humbling ourselves.

"[Humility is] the nothingness that makes room for God to prove His power," wrote Andrew Murray.[3] That is, the nothingness that makes room for God to prove His power by living His life in and through us as we just live.

> *Wholeness is because of oneness with Christ.*

The way we become the best is by dying the most while in these bodies living in this world. Dying is letting go and just living. He who dies the most before he dies wins because he who dies the most is the one through whom Christ lives the most (John 12:23–25). The one who counts on his or her oneness with Christ the most is the one through whom the indwelling Christ can live the most. Counting on my oneness with Christ = just living, and just living = counting on my oneness with Christ.

The one who wins is the one who is most humble because the one who wins is the one who knows most deeply that he no longer lives, but Christ lives in him. There's no room for pride with the winner because the winner knows he no longer lives, but Christ lives in and through him. There's no room for pride when we believe and live Galatians 2:20. We live Galatians 2:20 by just living because we believe that the Jesus living in us will be living through us as we just live, and He does, and thereby we bear "much fruit" and win.

"For the Lord bestows His blessing there, where He finds the vessels empty," wrote Thomas à Kempis in *Of the Imitation of Christ*.[4] In other words, the Lord fills up where He finds the vessel just living. We don't *try* to die. We die by just living. We just live because we know Christ will be living through us as we do so.

Andrew Murray put it this way: "The soul in which the wondrous combination of perfect passivity with the highest activity is most completely realized, has the deepest experience of what the Christian life is."[5] "Perfect passivity" = just living. Just living is because I believe that Christ Himself will indeed be filling and living through me as I'm doing so = experiential oneness with Christ = wholeness = where God is bringing us.

We Press On in Dying so We Can Know Christ Better

We press on in wanting to know Christ and the power of His resurrection. We press on in wanting to know in our own lives the power that comes from walking in, counting upon, and living out of the oneness with Christ that we already have. In other words we press on in abiding in the Vine so that we will experience the bearing of "much fruit" and glorify the Father.

At whatever level, to whatever degree, and for whatever reason we find ourselves fighting against, arguing with, and being afraid of just living is where God is working to free us from ourselves and give us Himself. Whatever within us is fighting against just living is what we need to let go of, what we need to die to. For it is God's will and purpose to bring us to the place of letting go and just living, and He is accomplishing this in us. It is God's will and purpose to bring us to this place of *knowing* the oneness with Christ that we already have (1 Corinthians 2:12) and therefore just living so He can live through us.

Wholeness is where God is bringing us. Wholeness = just living and just living = wholeness. Wholeness is because of oneness with Christ. God bringing us to this place of knowing and counting upon our oneness with Christ explains everything going on inside of us and in our lives. Knowing oneness with Christ, and thereby knowing freedom and wholeness, is where God is bringing us (John 8:32).

– 16 –

A Little More About Letting Go

PSALM 131

He who will ever cling to natural reasoning and ability in his journey to God will not become a very spiritual person.
—Attributed to St. John of the Cross

Many times in the previous pages I have used the term "letting go." Of course, I mean a deep, inward thing, a letting go of control at ever-deepening levels of our being as God brings us to those places and deals with them. For each of us, He does this in His perfect timing, in His perfect way. Letting go of control at ever-deepening levels of our being is a progressive thing. It is what sanctification is.

Children of God don't really believe that if they simply let go of striving and just live, that Christ really will fill in that inner space that is left, that He really will take over and begin filling and living through them more than He was before. In other words, we don't really believe that we are just a branch in a Vine. We don't really believe that it is no longer I who live, but Christ lives in me. Because we're not hearing the message enough (Romans 10:17), we don't really believe that Christ will live through us as we let go

157

of control and just live. But this *is* the truth, this *is* the way it is, this *is* what Scripture teaches.

We do want and try to control really deeply. It is perhaps our greatest "hidden fault." Much of our attempts at control have to do with leaning on our own understanding versus trusting in the Lord with *all* our heart (Proverbs 3:5). Much of what "letting go" is has to do with letting go of human reasoning and insisting upon understanding.

Think about this: If we were trusting in the Lord with *all* our heart, we would always be at peace. If we were trusting in the Lord with all our heart *about everything*, we would always be at peace. So the more we grow in faith, the closer we get to trusting in the Lord with all our heart, the more peace we will be experiencing. Inner peace will become our lifestyle.

We Idolize Human Reason and Wonder Why Our Souls Are Disquieted

> My heart is not proud, O LORD, my eyes are not haughty; I do not concern myself with great matters or things too wonderful for me. But I have stilled and quieted my soul; like a weaned child with its mother, like a weaned child is my soul within me. O Israel, put your hope in the LORD both now and forevermore. (Psalm 131)

David says in the psalm, "My heart is not proud, O LORD, my eyes are not haughty; I do not concern myself with great matters or things too wonderful for me." But we do—all the time. Haughtiness concerns itself with great matters and things too wonderful for it because it believes it can figure it out. Haughtiness limits God to the confines of its own created mind. Haughtiness doesn't realize that as the heavens are higher than the earth, so are God's ways higher than our ways and His thoughts than our thoughts (Isaiah 55:9).

Humility, which is simply seeing oneself accurately in relation to God, responds to the idea of great matters and things too wonderful for us by saying, "What isn't?! What isn't a great matter or too wonderful for me?!" Humility therefore trusts in the Lord with *all* its heart and leans not on its own understanding.

Let's look at the words of Jesus in John 9:39–41: "Jesus said, 'For judgment I have come into this world, so that the blind will see and those who see will become blind.' Some Pharisees who were with him heard him say this and asked, 'What? Are we blind too?' Jesus said, 'If you were blind, you would not be guilty of sin; but now that you claim you can see, your guilt remains.' "

Of course, Jesus is speaking of spiritual sight and blindness, spiritual understanding and its lack. We must learn to distrust our own abilities if we are to see spiritual truth. Scripture tells us where true wisdom and understanding are found:

No one knows the thoughts of God except the Spirit of God.
(1 Corinthians 2:11)

As the heavens are higher than the earth, so are my ways higher than your ways and my thoughts than your thoughts.
(Isaiah 55:9)

But it is the spirit (Spirit) in a man, the breath of the Almighty, that gives him understanding. (Job 32:8)

But the Counselor, the Holy Spirit, whom the Father will send in my name, will teach you all things and will remind you of everything I have said to you. (John 14:26)

But when he, the Spirit of truth, comes, he will guide you into all truth. (John 16:13)

As for you, the anointing you received from him remains in you, and you do not need anyone to teach you. But as his anointing teaches you about all things and as that anointing is real, not counterfeit—just as it has taught you, remain in him. (1 John 2:27)

Fénelon said of the Lord: "You are also inside us . . . in that inaccessible church and sanctuary of our souls. . . . It is there that are put to death all of our selfish desires, all of our self-interested turning inward upon ourselves, and all of our movements of self-love."[1]

This is a deep, loving work of God in us. Over time He causes us to let go of these initially unconscious, indwelling, harmful inward patterns and movements of self-love. This explains much of serious Christians' inward struggling and unease. It is a struggle to stay alive and hold onto control in the face of, at the same time, wanting to die, wanting to let go. It is a dying on the cross (Galatians 5:16–18). Thankfully, "the cross . . . always has its way" (Tozer), God always wins. This is His love that surpasses knowledge, that He would put us through this in order to free us from ourselves and give us Himself. We have been predestined to be conformed to the likeness of His Son. Jesus learned obedience from what He suffered, and so do we. Jesus learned letting go (not that He ever held on) from what He suffered, and so do we.

Thinking Is Overrated

So David confesses in Psalm 131:1, "My heart is not proud, O LORD, my eyes are not haughty. I do not concern myself with great matters or things too wonderful for me." As I said above, a good inward response to this statement would be "What isn't?" What isn't too wonderful for me to understand with my own reasoning when it comes to knowing God and His truth? We need to come to the humble, reasonable realization and conclusion that only God Himself can reveal truth to us if and when He chooses.

Human reasoning is overrated. Thinking is overrated. Our Western Christianity is more cognitive than spiritual . . . more head than heart . . . more faith in our thinking than living by faith. A. W. Tozer said, "The man taught by the Spirit of God will be a seer rather than a scholar," and yet we find too many in the church are more scholars than seers.[2]

> *We've replaced living by the Spirit with living by the head.*

In Psalm 139:17–18, David wrote, "How precious to me are your thoughts, O God! How vast is the sum of them! Were I to count them, they would outnumber the grains of sand." Of course, this is the same David who wrote Psalm 131, the same David who wrote, "My heart is not proud, O LORD, my eyes are not haughty; I do not concern myself with great matters or things too wonderful for me." This is the same David who wrote, "The LORD confides in those who fear him; he makes his covenant known to them" (Psalm 25:14). The covenant the Lord confides in the humble about and makes known to them is the New Covenant of the Spirit.

A prayer: "How precious to me are *your* thoughts, O God! How vast is the sum of them! O that instead of my own frantic, fear-driven, self-willed, prideful, compulsive thinking I would simply let go, wait, and listen as I slowly read and study Your Word, expecting You Yourself to speak to me, confide in me, show me truth in my heart (Ephesians 1:18–19) and make Your covenant known to me. I am blind. O that You Yourself would give me sight

(John 9:39–41). Please make me a seer of Your truth. Amen." See your Father's response to this prayer in Romans 8:32.

For the most part, we are the church at Ephesus Jesus is speaking to in Revelation 2. We have all our doctrinal ducks in a row but have left our first love. Love is the fruit of the Spirit. The reason we have left our first love is because we have left the Holy Spirit. The degree to which we leave the Holy Spirit is the degree to which we leave our first love.

What actions do we see described in the following two verses?

> I wait for the LORD, my soul waits, and in his word I put my hope. My soul waits for the LORD more than watchmen wait for the morning, more than watchmen wait for the morning.
> (Psalm 130:5–6)

> Much dreaming and many words are meaningless. Therefore stand in awe of God. (Ecclesiastes 5:7)

We need more humble waiting and less prideful thinking. We need more listening and less speaking. More waiting on the Lord and standing in awe and less trying to understand on our own. We need more living by the Spirit and less living by the head. To a significant degree, we've replaced living by the Spirit with living by the head. We need more just living and less living by the head.

Isn't this something we all do too much of? We concern ourselves with great matters and things of God and His ways that are too wonderful for us to understand. Rather than waiting on God to be our light, we inwardly insist on understanding now. We worry and fret. We lean on our own understanding. We fight against waiting on God. We fight against and resist the slow and obscure working of God and His grace and His keeping us in the darkness of faith for our own good. We must have the answer now.

The harder we try to understand and figure it out, the more oppressive it becomes (Psalm 73:16), but we feel compelled. In fact, this is the very indwelling sin area that God is choosing to work on and free us from. As with Asaph in Psalm 73, there is an apparent and frightening contradiction, and we insist on solving it in our heads, and we want to solve it *right now*. What is really going on is the outworking of a deeply rooted habit of insisting on a sense of control in the face of fear. Attempting to get and insisting upon control is the sin nature's response to fear. It is indwelling sin that only God can free us from, and the process is painful.

Letting Go Is Letting Go of Insistence on Understanding

Like a child being weaned, we must be made to "let go." The stronger our wills, the more we must be lovingly forced to let go. It is for our own good. It is God "weaning" us from a deeply rooted habit of leaning on our own understanding versus trusting Him with all our heart. Like the weaned child, God is actually bringing us to a place of greater freedom. Once we let go, there is a greater peace and rest and freedom to just live, like a weaned child with its mother. There is now an inner peace and freedom to just walk alongside, holding hands with, relaxed and at peace with Mom.

Interestingly, Asaph experienced the same relaxedness and inner peace when he finally let go, when he finally let go of insistence on knowing the answer. When Asaph let go of his anger and insistence on control in the presence of God, not only did he get the answer, but he found peace. He realized, "I am always with you; you hold me by my right hand [like the weaned child and Mom]. You guide me with your counsel, and afterward you will take me into glory" (Psalm 73:23–24). Of course, Asaph had all this even while he was behaving like a brute beast before God, but this knowledge of God and Asaph's relationship with Him became experiential after he let go, after he let go of his insistence on understanding and having the answer now.

Trusting in the Lord with all our hearts is a trusting in God Himself for who He is, a trusting in God and His character in the midst of inwardly painful wrestling, confusion, frustration, and seeming divine absence. It is hard to let go and trust in Someone's mere presence when He is feeling so absent. It feels like letting go into thin air, into nothingness, but it isn't.

> *All letting go is letting go to the Spirit because He is the one ruling in you now.*

"Yet I am always with you; you hold me by my right hand [like the weaned child's mother]. You guide me with your counsel, and afterward you will take me into glory" (Psalm 73:23–24).

Causing us to let go of control at ever-deepening levels of our being accurately interprets and explains much, if not all, of the inward struggle, frustration, and fretting we put ourselves through. See if this is not true about you. Be mindful of the fact that the next time you are struggling, wrestling, and discontent within, if not panicking, it is because in some form, at some level, you are insisting on control, and God is lovingly dealing with this inside of you. You will see this is the case. You want to think and figure it out, and He wants you to let go. Your sinful nature desires what is contrary to the Spirit, and the Spirit desires what is contrary to the sinful nature. What each desires is control (Galatians 5:16–18).

We Win Through Surrender

The answer to this Galatians 5:16–18 battle is letting go. The answer is in surrendering. All letting go is letting go to the Spirit because He is the one ruling in you now. He is the dominant force within you now. If you are led by the Spirit—and you are—you are not under law. So just yield, just let go, just surrender, just live. The Holy Spirit always fills in space created by brokenness with Himself. The Holy Spirit always fills in space created by letting go with Himself. Letting go = letting go of self-willed thinking = letting go of control = just living. Just living = letting go of control at ever-deepening levels of our being. "O Israel, put your hope in the LORD (living in you) both now and forevermore" (Psalm 131:3). For everything.

Proverbs 3:5 instructs, "Trust in the LORD with all your heart and lean not on your own understanding." Leaning on one's own understanding is just another form of trying to get control. Insistence on understanding is simply a way of trying to be in control. The problem with this is found in Isaiah 55:8–9, " 'For my thoughts are not your thoughts, neither are your ways my ways,' declares the LORD. 'As the heavens are higher than the earth, so are my ways higher than your ways and my thoughts than your thoughts.' " Therefore, the only solution is to be waiting on the Lord to give you His thoughts and to show you His ways and, in addition, trusting Him with all your heart when He is doing neither, like a weaned child with its mother.

A weaned child walking with his mother doesn't know her thoughts unless she tells him. Whether she does or not, the child still trusts her and her love.

"What, then, renders this soul so perfectly content?" wrote Jeanne Guyon. "It neither knows, nor wants to know, anything but what God calls it to."[3]

– 17 –

Keep in Step

MATTHEW 11:25–30

*While you labor less you will do many more useful things. It
is not a question of a perpetual struggle of the head.*
—Attributed to François Fénelon

Matthew 11:25–30 is another passage that will help us in our
understanding of what it means to be "letting go":

> At that time Jesus said, "I praise you, Father, Lord of heaven
> and earth, because you have hidden these things from the
> wise and learned, and revealed them to little children. Yes,
> Father, for this was your good pleasure. All things have
> been committed to me by my Father. No one knows the
> Son except the Father, and no one knows the Father except
> the Son and those to whom the Son chooses to reveal him.
> Come to me, all you who are weary and burdened, and I will
> give you rest. Take my yoke upon you and learn from me,
> for I am gentle and humble in heart, and you will find rest
> for your souls. For my yoke is easy and my burden is light."

What are "these things" that Jesus is speaking of that have been
hidden from the wise and learned and revealed to little children?

They would be the gospel and all of the things Jesus is speaking and teaching. The passages I have been quoting and explaining and the truths contained in them are "these things." The New Covenant of the Spirit, what freedom and union are, and what sanctification and the role of suffering in it is—these are "these things." The truth of living by the Spirit and the wholeness that comes as a result are "these things."

> *I wish we taught little children the truth of Jesus living through us as we just live.*

According to Jesus, even little children—*especially* little children—can "see" and understand and feel and be set free to just live by "these things." I wish we taught little children the truth of Jesus living through us as we just live. I wish we taught little children the lesson of the Vine and branches by showing them a bunch of grapes and explaining John 15:5 to them. They could understand it and start out their Christian life way ahead of, and more fruitful than, most of the adults around them.

Also, *we* are the little children. I am a little child. You are a little child. We can all have these things revealed to us by our Father. By God's grace and because the Son chooses to reveal the Father to us, all believers can know the Father and the Son more and more deeply and relationally. The truths in verses 28–30 are "these things" that the Father chooses to reveal to us, His children.

"How great is the love the Father has lavished on us, that we should be called children of God! And that is what we are!" (1 John 3:1).

Weary and Burdened from What?

Jesus says that all of us who are weary and burdened can come to Him and He will give us rest. Weary and burdened from what? Weary and burdened because of sin and enslavement to sin (John 8:34; Romans 7:24–25). Weary and burdened because of continually trying so hard not to sin and continually failing anyway (Romans 7:14–20). Weary and burdened from the ongoing battle within me between what I want to do and what I end up doing (Galatians 5:16–18). Weary and burdened from trying to keep the law and failing (Romans 7:14–25). Weary and burdened from trying to live the Christian life and do what the Bible says and not being able to do it.

Weary and burdened from just trying to live life in general. Weary and burdened from all the decisions, responsibilities, appointments, parenting, work stress, and technology stress. Weary and burdened from just trying to live life. Weary and burdened because life seems to take so much effort. I always have to be "working on" something to improve myself, my marriage, my parenting, my relationships with friends. Is life really meant to be so much effort?

Is Desiring and Expecting Wholeness Unreasonable and Irresponsible?

Is it too much to ask, is it unreasonable, is it irresponsible, to expect that I should be able to just live, to just be myself, and at the same time find that life is balanced and I'm being the person I'm needing and wanting to be and getting the things done I'm needing to get done without all the self-effort, self-recrimination, and striving? Am I asking too much in expecting that I should be able to just live, to just rest and be myself, and still be making good decisions and succeeding? (See Psalm 1).

In other words, is it too much to ask that I should be able to be just living and still be good and loving and other-centered? Is it too much to ask that I should be just living and still be who the Bible says I should be? Is this wholeness too much to ask for?

Jesus and the New Covenant of the Spirit say no, it is not too much to ask. In fact, all of this is where God is bringing us.

"Resting in Him as [my] utmost end" is how John Owen put it.[1] Resting in Him = abiding = just living. Therefore we can say, "Just living as my utmost end."

Jesus said to His followers, "If you hold to my teaching, you are really my disciples. Then you will know the truth, and the truth will set you free. . . . So if the Son sets you free, you will be free indeed" (John 8:31–32, 36).

Jesus Says the Christian Life Is Easy and Light

"Come to me, all you who are weary and burdened, and I will give you rest" (Matthew 11:28). Rest = just living and being Christlike at the same time. How does this happen?

Jesus continues in verses 29–30, "Take my yoke upon you and learn from me, for I am gentle and humble in heart, and you will find rest for your souls. For my yoke is easy and my burden is light"—as opposed to the burden we put on ourselves and the burden others put on us. Jesus said to the experts in the law, "Woe to you, because you load people down with burdens they can hardly carry, and you yourselves will not lift one finger to help them" (Luke 11:46).

According to Jesus, His yoke is easy and His burden is light. When it comes to living the Christian life, any yoke that is hard and any burden that is heavy are not Jesus's yoke or burden. It must be ours that we laid on ourselves or someone else's that they laid on us. We learn false burdens. Others put heavy burdens on us by things they say and teach. These things are not truthful. The truth always has the effect of setting us free (John 8:32). The world, the worldly, the sin nature, and the devil teach us wrong things that burden us. Pharisees teach us right things without teaching us the truth about how these things are accomplished in our lives.

We Must Learn from the Old Ox and the Farmer

In Jesus's day, the way a farmer trained a young, inexperienced ox was to yoke him up with an older, experienced ox. They were yoked together, and the farmer started them down the rows of the field. The old ox had been up and down the rows a hundred times, maybe more. He knew the way. Now this young ox was often willful, stubborn, uncomfortable, and wanting to do things his own way. The young ox would pull at the yoke to go faster or slower or in a whole different direction. He would push and pull and strain at the yoke. Sometimes the farmer had to goad him. He had to inflict pain with a sharp instrument to discipline the young ox and make him calm down and just walk alongside the old ox. He had to break the will of the young ox. The young ox was bothered, upset, stressed, and in pain as long as he kept on insisting on his own way and trying to be independent and control things.

Finally, when the young ox simply lowered his head and yielded to the leading of the old ox, either because he was exhausted or because he was finally responding to discipline, there was peace, outwardly and inwardly, and he got a whole lot more done too.

The young ox was restful and content as he just surrendered his will and let himself be controlled and led by the old ox. All of this was accomplished because the young ox chose to keep in step with the old ox. He was restful and content and fruitful by simply yielding to the oneness relationship he already had with the old ox. The young ox could rest. He could just live and be content, fruitful and much more effective than he had been before. Living in oneness with the old ox was restful, fruitful, and normal life all at the same time, and it was "easy," certainly easier than the self-willed life he was living before. Surrendering to oneness with Himself and just living is what Jesus is teaching here.

Matthew 11:25–30; Galatians 5:25–26; Romans 6:11–23; and John 15:5 Inform and Explain One Another

This is what Jesus is teaching with this analogy. It is what He means by it. Of course you see the comparisons . . . the old ox is the Holy Spirit, the one who is in control now, to whom all we need do is yield. The diagram would be helpful at this point (see p. 49). You and I, the Christians, are the young, inexperienced ox. We must take His yoke upon us and learn from Him. We must simply inwardly let go of control and yield to the indwelling, filling, controlling old ox living inside of us. We find rest for our souls only as we let go and just live, utterly depending on and counting on our oneness with Jesus now, our oneness with the indwelling, filling, controlling Holy Spirit. The result will be rest and bearing much fruit. His yoke is easy and His burden is light because of oneness with Him.

The apostle Paul wrote, "Since we live by the Spirit, let us keep in step with the Spirit. Let us not become conceited, provoking and envying each other" (Galatians 5:25–26). What Paul means by keeping in step with the Spirit is perfectly explained and clarified by Matthew 11:28–30.

Also, please notice that what Paul is saying in Galatians 5:25–26 is that the way we keep from becoming conceited and provoking and envying each other is by keeping in step with the Spirit. The church will not love one another the way it should until it learns deeply what it means to live by the Spirit and to keep in step with the Spirit. Keeping in step with the Spirit is the only way we will love one another.

In Matthew 11:28–30, Jesus teaches about a deep, inward thing, an "inmost being" thing; He is teaching about letting go and faith. Matthew 11:28–30 is about what "letting go" is . . . it is a letting go of control at whatever level of our being we are still holding onto it and insisting upon it. It is a letting go to the gracious controlling One with whom we are now one.

> *It is not unreasonable to realize that all you are able to be is a branch.*

Matthew 11:28–30 is what Paul is teaching in Romans 6:11–23. Paul uses the analogy of slavery and simply yielding to what is (see the diagram on page 49) in the same way Jesus is using the analogy of being yoked to Him now and free from the burdens of sin, the law, and self-effort. Both Paul and Jesus are teaching the same truth. Both Paul and Jesus are teaching rest and fruit in our lives as the norm as we just live because of actual real oneness with the resurrected Christ by His Spirit. And both of these analogies, being yoked and being enslaved, are teaching the same truth as being a branch in the Vine (John 15:5).

A branch just lives and thereby is greatly lived through and bears much fruit. It is not unreasonable or irresponsible to want to just be a branch, especially since that is what we already are. It is prideful to think we are anything more, and we only end up hindering God's working through us when we try to be anything more. It is not unreasonable or irresponsible to finally realize and acknowledge that all you are able to be is a branch. It is not unreasonable or irresponsible to want to be free to just live. It is not unreasonable or irresponsible to let go and just live because of genuinely expecting that Jesus Himself will be living through you as you do so. It is living in reality.

It is not unreasonable or irresponsible to not be willing to settle for anything less than perfect experiential oneness with

Christ = wholeness = perfect rest and much fruit at the same time because of Jesus living through you as you just live. It is not unreasonable or irresponsible to expect that we should be able to just live and find ourselves being good and fruitful and righteous as the norm at the same time. It is not unreasonable or irresponsible . . . it is the life of faith . . . it is what we are called to . . . it is where God is bringing us for His glory and our joy. "Just a branch" is who and what we must be and the place we must come to as Christians if we are going to persevere in these last days and change the world around us. Jesus can do it better than we can . . . die so He can do it. Dying = just living. His strength will be made perfect in your weakness; He will live through you as you just live.

As with the young ox, suffering in the form of God's patient disciplining us and causing or permitting pain in our lives is all for the purpose of causing us to die to self, all for the purpose of causing us to let go of self-will and control at ever-deepening levels of our being so that we can become more like the old ox, so that we can be further conformed to the likeness of Jesus. Yielding to the old ox = becoming like Jesus in His death = letting go = "and so, somehow," attaining to the resurrection from the dead more and more in this life.

– 18 –

A Final Word on Just Living

Let everything become silent that is not You.
—François Fénelon

Just living, like letting go and dying to self, has a lot to do with letting go of our bad habits of too much self-willed thinking and leaning on our own understanding (Proverbs 3:5–6; Psalm 131). God will be working in us, causing us to come to this place of letting go and just living. This often explains what is going on inside of you when you find yourself struggling inwardly. It makes no sense to be trying to figure things out with your head when God is testing your heart to see if you'll just trust Him.

"It is the will of God that we should be ignorant," Fénelon claimed. "It is trifling by the way to reason about the way."[1]

Proverbs 20:24 tells us, "A man's steps are directed by the LORD. How then can anyone understand his own way?" To this I would add, "So quit trying so much."

A Holy Unthinking

It is the heart which experiences God, and not the reason.
This, then, is faith: God felt by the heart, not by the reason.
—Blaise Pascal

[Faith is] the proper and fitting means of union with God.
—St. John of the Cross

*Thus [the soul] approaches God more nearly by not
understanding than by understanding.*
—St. John of the Cross

There must be a holy unthinking involved in living by faith because God says to us, "For my thoughts are not your thoughts, neither are your ways my ways. . . . As the heavens are higher than the earth, so are my ways higher than your ways and my thoughts than your thoughts" (Isaiah 55:8–9). That is immensely higher, and thereby immensely different, than our own self-willed thinking and limited reasoning. His thoughts shared with us by His Spirit through His Word are better.

> *Fénelon said, "True knowledge . . . is only open to those who distrust their own abilities."*

Fénelon said, "True knowledge . . . is only open to those who distrust their own abilities; proud human wisdom is unworthy to be taken into the counsels of God. God renders the working of grace slow and obscure, then, so that he may keep us in the darkness of faith."[2]

In volume 2, we will be reviewing Romans 6–8 in depth, but for now let me leave you with this one verse: "The mind of sinful man is death, but the mind controlled by the Spirit is life and peace" (Romans 8:6). Self-willed compulsive thinking is characterized by anxiety and "oppression" (Psalm 73:16). The mind controlled by the Spirit as we're just living is life and peace.

You can know that whenever your thinking is resulting in anxiety and increasing frustration, you've crossed over from being yielded to God and just living to self-will and insistence on control. This can be quite subtle, but not so subtle that you won't know when you're doing it. It will only get worse until you finally let go and just live, because the Holy Spirit who lives in you always fills with Himself the space created by your letting go.

God is able and willing to show us what we need to see as and when we need to see it . . . so just live. As children of His, our good Father will discipline us as and when we need it. He is more interested in sanctifying us and conforming us to the likeness of His Son than we are. The "one thing needed" is receiving from Him (Luke 10:38–42). We need not be worried and upset about self. Rather, let's count ourselves dead to sin but alive to God in Christ Jesus.

We walk in the light. We walk in openness to God's revealing sin to us when it is there (Psalm 139:23–24). We count on it. Believing He will do this frees us to just live. When and as He shows us, we confess and thank Him for His forgiveness, and we keep going. We trust Him to show us our sin, as and when we need to see it. As and when we see it, we confess, we acknowledge our sin, we keep current. We walk in the light, counting ourselves "dead to sin but alive to God in Christ Jesus," trusting our loving Father to show us what we need to see as and when we need to see it.

Just living = living by confidence in our oneness with Christ = living by the Spirit = freedom and wholeness = where God is bringing us.

Favorite Quotes

Faith

"For true faith, it is either God or total collapse."

—A. W. Tozer[1]

"Great faith produces great abandonment."

—Jeanne Guyon[2]

"The heart has its reasons, of which
reason does not know."

—Blaise Pascal[3]

"We can learn nothing of the gospel except by feeling its
truths. . . . There are some sciences that may be learned by
the head, but the science of Christ crucified can only be
learned by the heart."

—Charles Spurgeon[4]

"True knowledge . . . is only open to those who distrust
their own abilities; proud human wisdom is unworthy to be
taken into the counsels of God. God renders the working of
grace slow and obscure, then, so that he may keep us in the
darkness of faith."

—François Fénelon[5]

"What, then, renders this soul so perfectly content?
It neither knows, nor wants to know, anything but
what God calls it to."

—Jeanne Guyon[6]

"There are those learned opinions which are more fastidious than correct, more plausible than true."

—Attributed to Charles Spurgeon[7]

"Unbelief: 'He can't be that good!' → Independence from God/Dependence on Self."

—Attributed to Larry Crabb[8]

"Naked faith, alone, is a sure guard against illusion."

—François Fénelon[9]

The Holy Spirit's Filling

"How do you convince a world that God is alive? By His aliveness in your life, by His work in producing reality in your experience. What a message for a phony generation."

—Howard Hendricks[10]

"It is not a great stir in the realm of fleshly doing but a divine dying which will bring the church again to a flaming apostolic zeal . . . and to a fruitfulness comparable to that of the earliest Christians."

—F. J. Huegel[11]

"God is not looking for people to work for Him but people who let Him work mightily in and through them."

—John Piper[12]

"What lies behind us and what lies before us are small
matters compared to what lies within us."

—Henry Stanley Haskins[13]

"Where God finds space he enters."

—Larry Crabb[14]

"The LORD confides in those who fear him;
he makes his covenant known to them."

—Psalm 25:14

Oneness with Christ

"The soul in which the wondrous combination of perfect
passivity with the highest activity is most completely
realized, has the deepest experience
of what the Christian life is."

—Andrew Murray[15]

"I have been crucified with Christ and I no longer live,
but Christ lives in me. The life I now live in the body,
I live by faith in the Son of God, who loved me
and gave himself for me."

—Galatians 2:20

"I will walk about in freedom, for I have
sought out your precepts."

—Psalm 119:45

"If God wishes to show you more, he will be your light;
you need none but him."

—Julian of Norwich[16]

"All Christ's teaching of His disciples, and all their vain
efforts, were the needful preparation for His entering into
them in divine power, to give and be in them what He had
taught them to desire."

—Andrew Murray[17]

"When we are humbly prepared to make the fact of our
death with Christ our daily basis of life and service, there is
nothing that can prevent the uprising and outflow of new
life, . . . and meet the need of thirsty souls around us."

—J. C. Metcalfe[18]

"Religious experience for Paul is basically
experience of union with Christ."

—J. D. G. Dunn[19]

"While you labor less, you will do many more
useful things. It is not a question of a perpetual
struggle of the head."

—François Fénelon[20]

"[The Christian life] is *not* an imitation of Christ.
It is a participation in Christ."

—F. J. Huegel[21]

"For as in his incarnation he took our nature into personal
union with his own; so herein he takes our persons into a
mystical union with Himself."

—John Owen[22]

"There is not a New Testament requirement that does not immediately bring the believer face to face with an overwhelming dilemma. Either he must cease to move in the realm of the purely natural—die to the 'flesh-life' and find in the resurrected Christ a new life—or he must fail as a Christian. To the new life—the life that flows from Christ— the Sermon on the Mount presents no problems."

—F. J. Huegel[23]

"This principle of participation—oneness with Christ—has reaches so unfathomable that not even the spiritual man finds it easy to scale the heights and grasp its full meaning. We stand overawed. We stagger. Faith wavers."

—F. J. Huegel[24]

"Christ came . . . not to get us doing, but to bring us to an undoing."

—L. E. Maxwell[25]

"We must hope [for] nothing [from] self, but wait for everything from God."

—François Fénelon[26]

"Resting in Him as [my] utmost end."

—John Owen[27]

"If godliness is not from deep inside you, it is only a mask."

—Jeanne Guyon[28]

"God, help me to believe the truth about myself, no matter how beautiful it may be."

—Macrina Wiederkehr[29]

"It is there [inside of us] that the Word made flesh gives Himself to us as our inner word, as our promise, our wisdom, our life, our being, our all."

—François Fénelon[30]

"The will of God has nothing but sweetness, favours and treasures for submissive souls; it is impossible to repose too much confidence in it, nor to abandon oneself to it too utterly."

—Jean-Pierre de Caussade[31]

"Happy are those whose mind contains only what is necessary, and who think of nothing except when it is time to think of it."

—François Fénelon[32]

"Inner peace does not exist except for the humble."

—François Fénelon[33]

"The New Covenant was given to make it possible for me to live with God as my deepest desire."

—Larry Crabb[34]

Sanctification and Suffering

"Receive everything that God presents to your mind, notwithstanding the shrinking of nature, as a trial by which He would exercise and strengthen your faith."

—François Fénelon[35]

"What is man that you make so much of him, that you give him so much attention, that you examine him every morning and test him every moment? Will you never look away from me, or let me alone even for an instant?"

—Job 7:17–19

"We may be assured, that there is an internal [spiritual] advancement, where there is an advancement in the way of the cross. Abandonment [to Christ] and the Cross go hand in hand."

—Jeanne Guyon[36]

"The fullness of joy is seeing God in all things."

—Julian of Norwich[37]

"Your sufferings, your actions, your attractions are the species under which God gives Himself to you, while you are vainly striving after sublime ideas."

—Jean-Pierre de Caussade[38]

"Man rises up with all his power to plead against a conviction of impotency."

—John Owen[39]

"It is enough to be humbled and abandoned [to God] in the midst of suffering."

—François Fénelon[40]

"The only sure mark of the presence of God [is] the disappearance of self."

—Andrew Murray[41]

"But this victory is achieved only through death,
for the 'self-life' and the satanic spirit are
in unconscious affinity."

—F. J. Huegel[42]

"Think you it is nothing to repress all the uneasy reflections
of self-love; to press forward continually without knowing
whither we go, and yet without stopping?"

—François Fénelon[43]

"The goal of sanctification is 'entire crucifixion
to the habits of the life of self.'"

—François Fénelon[44]

"In places we don't choose, You make all things new."

—"Father, Let Your Kingdom Come"[45]

"Brokenness allows us to relax in the arms
that will bring us to shore."

—Larry Crabb[46]

"It is the fire of suffering which will bring forth
the gold of godliness."

—Jeanne Guyon[47]

"You are also inside us . . . in that inaccessible church and
sanctuary of our souls. . . . It is there that are put to death all
of our selfish desires, all of our self-interested turning inward
upon ourselves, and all of our movements of self-love."

—François Fénelon[48]

"Children of God—and everyone else—think nobody loves them enough for them to let go of control."

—Larry Crabb[49]

"Hadst Thou, O my God, spared the strokes of Thy hammer, I should never have been formed to Thy will, to be an instrument for Thy use; for I was ridiculously vain."

—Jeanne Guyon[50]

"Whatever light, whatever feeling we may possess, is all a delusion, if it lead us not to the real and constant practice of dying to self."

—François Fénelon[51]

Notes

1. God's Plan to Reach the Nations

1. A. W. Tozer, *The Root of the Righteous* (Moody, 1986), 58.
2. Andrew Murray, *Humility: The Journey Toward Holiness* (Bethany House, 2001), 48.
3. Murray, *Humility*, 48.
4. Howard Hendricks, *Elijah: Battle of the Gods* (Moody, 1979).

2. God's New Way

1. Thomas à Kempis, *Of the Imitation of Christ*, Chapter XV, Christian Classics Ethereal Library, https://www.ccel.org/k/kempis/imitation/formats/imitation-baker.html.
2. John Piper, *Brothers, We Are Not Professionals: A Plea to Pastors for Radical Ministry*, revised and expanded (B&H Publishing, 2013), 56.
3. Gene Edwards, *100 Days in the Secret Place: Classic Writings from Jeanne Guyon, François Fénelon, & Michael Molinos on the Deeper Christian Life* (Destiny Image, 2015), 63.

3. How Can This Be?

1. Jim Daly, "Ten Quotes That Can Change Your Life," Focus on the Family, https://jimdaly.focusonthefamily.com/ten-quotes-that-can-change-your-life/.
2. From the author's records. Unable to verify source.
3. F. J. Huegel, *Bone of His Bone* (CLC Publications, 1982), 62.

4. We Already Have It, We Just Need to Know It

1. From the author's records. Unable to verify source.
2. F. J. Huegel, *Bone of His Bone* (CLC Publications, 1982), 76.
3. John Owen, *Communion with God* (Reformation Heritage Books, 2014), 28.

5. Running in the Path of His Commands

1. Jeanne Guyon, *A Short and Easy Method of Prayer*, Christian Classics Ethereal Library, https://ccel.org/ccel/guyon/prayer.viii.html.
2. Andrew Murray, *Humility* (General Press, 2019), 46.
3. A. W. Tozer, *The Radical Cross* (Moody, 2009), 14.
4. Andrew Murray, "In Stillness of Soul," Bible Jesus, https://biblejesus.com/in-stillness-of-soul-andrew-murray/.
5. Julian of Norwich, *Showings* (Long Text), 193. Purdue University Fort Wayne, chrome-extension://efaidnbmnnnibpcajpcglclefind mkaj/https://users.pfw.edu/flemingd/JulianLongText.pdf.

6. Free Indeed

1. Blaise Pascal, *Pascal's Pensées* (E. P. Dutton & Co., 1958), 78. Project Gutenberg, https://www.gutenberg.org/files/18269/18269-h/18269-h.htm.

9. Gracious Affliction

1. Andrew Murray, *Humility* (General Press, 2019), 54.
2. Murray, *Humility*, 37.
3. F. J. Huegel, *Bone of His Bone: Going Beyond the Imitation of Christ* (CLC Publications, 1982), 62.
4. François Fénelon, Letter IV "The Death of Self," Christian Classics Ethereal Library, https://ccel.org/ccel/fenelon/progress/progress.iv.v.html.
5. From the author's records. Unable to verify source.
6. Jean-Pierre de Caussade, *Abandonment to Divine Providence*, Section VII, "On the Attainment of Peace," Christian Classics Ethereal Library, https://www.ccel.org/d/decaussade/abandonment/cache/abandonment.pdf.

10. What Paul Wants

1. This is a paraphrase of Fénelon. The original reads: "It is practised by continually losing our own will in the will of God; renouncing every private inclination as soon as it arises, however good it may appear, that we may stand in indifference with respect to ourselves, and only will what God has willed from all eternity," *Spiritual*

Progress, Christian Classics Ethereal Library, https://ccel.org /ccel/f/fenelon/progress/cache/progress.pdf.

2. Larry Crabb, *Shattered Dreams: God's Unexpected Path to Joy* (Waterbrook, 2010), 131.

3. Jean-Pierre de Caussade, *Abandonment to Divine Providence*, Book 2, Chapter III, Section V: "The Life of Faith," Christian Classics Ethereal Library, chrome-extension://efaidnbmnnnibpcajpcglclefindmkaj /https://www.ccel.org/d/decaussade/abandonment/cache /abandonment.pdf.

4. From the author's records. Unable to verify source.

5. This is a paraphrase of Fénelon. See note 1 above.

6. James Strong, *The New Strong's Expanded Dictionary of Bible Words,* (Nashville: Thomas Nelson Publishers, 2001), 1191.

12. Dying Inwardly

1. Jean-Pierre de Caussade, *Abandonment to Divine Providence,* Section VII, "On the Attainment of Peace," Christian Classics Ethereal Library, https://www.ccel.org/d/decaussade/abandonment /cache/abandonment.pdf.

2. A. W. Tozer, *The Radical Cross* (Moody, 2009), 14.

3. Jeanne Guyon, *Short and Easy Method of Prayer*, Chapter VII, "Of Sufferings," Christian Classics Ethereal Library, https://www.ccel .org/ccel/guyon/prayer.ix.html.

4. Larry Crabb, *Shattered Dreams: God's Unexpected Path to Joy* (Waterbrook, 2010), 104.

5. Crabb, *Shattered Dreams*, 102.

6. François Fénelon, *The Complete Fénelon* (Paraclete, 2008), quoted on Fr. Thomas Hopko, "Speaking the Truth in Love," Ancient Faith Ministries, March 20, 2014, https://www.ancientfaith.com /podcasts/hopko/archbishop_fenelon_and_great_lent/.

7. From the author's records. Unable to verify source.

8. "Father, Let Your Kingdom Come," by Ben Cooper, Madison Cunningham, Orlando Palmer, Latifah Phillips, Elizabeth Vice, Isaac Wardell, and Paul Zach, Hymns from the Porter's Gate Publishing (2017).

9. Crabb, *Shattered Dreams*, 107.

10. François Fénelon, *Spiritual Progress*, Chapter XXX, "On True Liberty," Christian Classics Ethereal Library, https://ccel.org /ccel/f/fenelon/progress/cache/progress.pdf.

13. And So Do We

1. *New International Version Study Bible* (Zondervan, 1978, revised 1983), 1864.
2. From the author's records. Unable to verify source.
3. F. J. Huegel, *Bone of His Bone: Going Beyond the Imitation of Christ* (CLC Publications, 1982), 65.
4. Karolina W. Sandell-Berg, "Day by Day," trans. Andrew L. Skoog, Hymnary.org, https://hymnary.org/text/day_by_day_and_with _each_passing_moment/fulltexts.
5. Jean-Pierre de Caussade, *Abandonment to Divine Providence*, 27, Christian Classics Ethereal Library, https://ccel.org/d /decaussade/abandonment/cache/abandonment.pdf.
6. Larry Crabb, *Connecting: Healing for Ourselves and Our Relationships* (Word, 1997), 15.
7. From the author's records. Unable to verify source.
8. Jeanne Guyon, *Autobiography of Madame Guyon*, Chapter 18, Christian Classics Ethereal Library, https://ccel.org/ccel/guyon /auto/auto.iii.xviii.html.
9. François Fénelon, *Spiritual Progress*, Letter IV, "The Death of Self," Christian Classics Ethereal Library, https://ccel.org/ccel/f /fenelon/progress/cache/progress.pdf.
10. François Fénelon, *Spiritual Letters*, #81 "How to Do All in the Spirit of Prayer," found on Internet Archive, https://ia801307.us.archive .org/2/items/spiritualletters00fnel_0/spiritualletters00fnel_0 .pdf.
11. Attributed to Julian of Norwich from the author's records. Unable to verify source.
12. From the author's records. Unable to verify source.

14. His Love That Surpasses Knowledge

1. François Fénelon, *Spiritual Letters*, Chapter 38, "The Life of Peace," found on Internet Archive, https://ia801307.us.archive.org/2 /items/spiritualletters00fnel_0/spiritualletters00fnel_0.pdf.

2. John Owen, *Communion with God* (Reformation Heritage Books, 2014), 28.
3. From the author's records. Unable to verify source.
4. Adaptation of a quotation from Julian of Norwich: "The fullness of joy is seeing God in all things."
5. A. W. Tozer, *The Radical Cross* (Moody, 2009), 14.
6. François Fénelon, *Spiritual Progress*, Letter IV, "The Death of Self," Christian Classics Ethereal Library, https://ccel.org/ccel/fenelon/progress/progress.iv.v.html.
7. Adaptation of a quotation from Julian of Norwich: "The fullness of joy is seeing God in all things."
8. François Fénelon, *Spiritual Progress*, Letter XII, "On Wandering Thoughts and Dejection," Christian Classics Ethereal Library, https://ccel.org/ccel/f/fenelon/progress/cache/progress.pdf.
9. Larry Crabb, *Soul Talk: The Language God Longs for Us to Speak* (Integrity, 2003), 134.

15. Press On . . . In What?

1. L. E. Maxwell, *Born Crucified* (Moody, 2010), 75.
2. J. D. G. Dunn, *Unity and Diversity in the New Testament: An Inquiry into the Character of Earliest Christianity* (SCM Press, 2006), 210.
3. Andrew Murray, *Humility* (General Press, 2019), 46.
4. Thomas à Kempis, *Of the Imitation of Christ*, Chapter XV, Christian Classics Ethereal Library, https://www.ccel.org/k/kempis/imitation/formats/imitation-baker.html.
5. Andrew Murray, "In Stillness of Soul," Bible Jesus, https://biblejesus.com/in-stillness-of-soul-andrew-murray/.

16. A Little More About Letting Go

1. From the author's records. Unable to verify source.
2. A. W. Tozer, *Man: The Dwelling Place of God* (Eldric Editions, 2025), 121.
3. Jeanne Guyon, *Autobiography of Madame Guyon*, Chapter 18, Christian Classics Ethereal Library, https://ccel.org/ccel/guyon/auto/auto.iii.xviii.html.

17. Keep in Step

1. John Owen, *Communion with God* (Reformation Heritage Books, 2014), 28.

18. A Final Word on Just Living

1. François Fénelon, *Spiritual Progress*, Chapter VII, "On Prayer," Christian Classics Ethereal Library, https://ccel.org/ccel/fenelon/progress/progress.iii.viii.html.
2. François Fénelon, *Spiritual Progress*, Chapter XXI, "On the Proper Use of Crosses," Christian Classics Ethereal Library, https://ccel.org/ccel/fenelon/progress/progress.iii.xxii.html.

Favorite Quotes

1. A. W. Tozer, *The Root of the Righteous* (Moody, 1986), 58.
2. Jeanne Guyon, *A Short and Easy Method of Prayer*, Chapter VI, "Of Self-Surrender," Christian Classics Ethereal Library, https://ccel.org/ccel/guyon/prayer.viii.html.
3. Blaise Pascal, *Pascal's Pensées* (E. P. Dutton & Co., 1958), 78. Project Gutenberg, https://www.gutenberg.org/files/18269/18269-h/18269-h.htm.
4. Charles Spurgeon, "The Evil and Its Remedy," Spurgeon Center, https://www.spurgeon.org/resource-library/sermons/the-evil-and-its-remedy/.
5. François Fénelon, *Spiritual Progress*, Chapter XXI, "On the Proper Use of Crosses," Christian Classics Ethereal Library, https://ccel.org/ccel/fenelon/progress/progress.iii.xxii.html.
6. Jeanne Guyon, *Autobiography of Madame Guyon*, Chapter 18, Christian Classics Ethereal Library, https://ccel.org/ccel/guyon/auto/auto.iii.xviii.html.
7. Attributed to Charles Spurgeon from the author's records. Unable to verify source.
8. Attributed to Larry Crabb from the author's records. Unable to verify source.
9. François Fénelon, *Spiritual Progress*, Chapter XXIV, "The Way of Naked Faith and Pure Love Is Better and More Certain Than That of Illuminations and Sensible Delights," Christian Classics Ethereal

Library, https://ccel.org/ccel/fenelon/progress/progress.iii.xxv
.html.

10. Howard Hendricks, *Elijah: Battle of the Gods* (Moody, 1979).

11. F. J. Huegel, *Bone of His Bone: Going Beyond the Imitation of Christ* (CLC Publications, 1982), 29.

12. John Piper, *Brothers, We Are Not Professionals: A Plea to Pastors for Radical Ministry*, updated and expanded (B&H Publishing Group, 2013), 56.

13. Often misattributed to Ralph Waldo Emerson, this quotation is actually from Henry Stanley Haskins, *Meditations in Wall Street* (W. Morrow and Co., 1940).

14. Larry Crabb, *Shattered Dreams: God's Unexpected Path to Joy*, (Colorado Springs: Waterbrook, 2010), 102.

15. Andrew Murray, "In Stillness of Soul," Bible Jesus, https://biblejesus.com/in-stillness-of-soul-andrew-murray/.

16. Julian of Norwich, *Turning to the Mystics*, Session 1 with James Finley, 2. Center for Action and Contemplation, chrome-extension://efaidnbmnnnibpcajpcglclefindmkaj/https://cac.org/wp-content/uploads/2022/09/TTTM_Transcript_JON_S1.pdf

17. Andrew Murray, *Humility: The Journey Toward Holiness* (Bethany House, 2001), 48.

18. J. C. Metcalfe, "The Rest of Faith," Grace Notebook, https://gracenotebook.com/the-rest-of-faith/.

19. J. D. G. Dunn, *Unity and Diversity in the New Testament: An Inquiry into the Character of Earliest Christianity* (SCM Press, 2006), 210.

20. François Fénelon from the author's records. Unable to verify source.

21. Huegel, *Bone of His Bone*, 18.

22. John Owen, *The Glory of Christ*, Chapter X, "The Glory of Christ in the Communication of Himself unto Believers," Christian Classics Ethereal Library, https://ccel.org/ccel/owen/glory/glory.i.xiii.html.

23. Huegel, *Bone of His Bone*, 62.

24. Huegel, *Bone of His Bone*, 65.

25. L. E. Maxwell, *Born Crucified* (Moody, 2010), 75.

26. François Fénelon, *Spiritual Progress*, Chapter VI, "On Humility," Christian Classics Ethereal Library, https://ccel.org/ccel/fenelon/progress/progress.iii.vii.html.

27. John Owen, *Communion With God* (Reformation Heritage Books, 2014), 28
28. Jeanne Guyon, quoted in Gene Edwards, *100 Days in the Secret Place: Classic Writings from Jeanne Guyon, François Fénelon, & Michael Molinos on the Deeper Christian Life* (Destiny Image, 2015), 63.
29. Macrina Wiederkehr, quoted in M. J. Ryan, *A Grateful Heart: Daily Blessings for the Evening Meals from Buddha to the Beatles* (Mango Media, 1994).
30. François Fénelon from the author's records. Unable to verify source.
31. Jean-Pierre de Caussade, *Abandonment to Divine Providence*, 27, Christian Classics Ethereal Library, https://ccel.org/d/decaussade/abandonment/cache/abandonment.pdf.
32. François Fénelon from the author's records. Unable to verify source.
33. François Fénelon from the author's records. Unable to verify source.
34. Larry Crabb from the author's records. Unable to verify source.
35. François Fénelon, *Spiritual Progress*, Letter XII, "On Wandering Thoughts and Dejection," 38, Christian Classics Ethereal Library, https://ccel.org/ccel/f/fenelon/progress/cache/progress.pdf.
36. Jeanne Guyon, *Short and Easy Method of Prayer*, chapter VII, "Of Sufferings," Christian Classics Ethereal Library, https://www.ccel.org/ccel/guyon/prayer.ix.html.
37. Julian of Norwich from the author's records. Unable to verify source.
38. Jean-Pierre de Caussade, *Abandonment to Divine Providence*, Book 2, Chapter III, Section V, "The Life of Faith," Christian Classics Ethereal Library, chrome-extension://efaidnbmnnnibpcajpcglclefindmkaj/https://www.ccel.org/d/decaussade/abandonment/cache/abandonment.pdf.
39. Owen, *Communion with God*, 87.
40. François Fénelon, *Spiritual Progress*, Chapter XXVIII, "Pure Love Only Can Suffer Aright and Love Its Sufferings," Christian Classics Ethereal Library, https://ccel.org/ccel/fenelon/progress/progress.iii.xxix.html.
41. Murray, *Humility*, 54.
42. Huegel, *Bone of His Bone*, 76.

43. François Fénelon, *Spiritual Progress*, Chapter VII, "On Prayer," Christian Classics Ethereal Library, https://ccel.org/ccel/fenelon/progress/progress.iii.viii.html.

44. François Fénelon from the author's records. Unable to verify source.

45. "Father, Let Your Kingdom Come," by Ben Cooper, Madison Cunningham, Orlando Palmer, Latifah Phillips, Elizabeth Vice, Isaac Wardell, and Paul Zach, Hymns from the Porter's Gate Publishing (2017).

46. Larry Crabb from the author's records. Unable to verify source.

47. Jeanne Guyon from the author's records. Unable to verify source.

48. François Fénelon from the author's records. Unable to verify source.

49. Larry Crabb, *Soul Talk: The Language God Longs for Us to Speak* (Integrity, 2003), 134.

50. Jeanne Guyon, *Autobiography of Madame Guyon*, Chapter 18, Christian Classics Ethereal Library, https://ccel.org/ccel/guyon/auto/auto.iii.xviii.html.

51. François Fénelon, Spiritual Progress, Letter IV "The Death of Self," Christian Classics Ethereal Library, https://ccel.org/ccel/fenelon/progress/progress.iv.v.html